CHILDREN AND WORK

CHILDREN AND WORK
A STUDY OF SOCIALIZATION

Bernard Goldstein
Jack Oldham

Transaction Books
New Brunswick, New Jersey

Library of Congress Catalog Number: 78-62894
ISBN: 0-87855-285-5
Printed in the United States of America

Library of Congress Cataloging in Publication Data

Goldstein, Bernard, 1925
  Children and Work.

  Bibliography: p.
  Includes index.
  1. Work. 2. Child development. 3. Socialization. 4. Vocational
interests. I. Oldham, Jack, 1947- joint author. II. Title.
HQ 784.W6G64 301.15'72 78-62894
ISBN 0-87855-285-5

Contents

List of Tables

Acknowledgements

A research project of this magnitude requires assistance from many people. The study could not have been conducted without the understanding and support of officials from a number of school districts and schools in New Jersey. We are grateful to them, their teachers, and the students who participated in the study, and regret that the pledge of anonymity prevents us from thanking them all in a more personal way.

We would like to express our appreciation, as well, to those listed below, each of whom contributed in an important way to making this study possible:

Graduate Research Assistants:
Barbara Held   Michael Zimmerman
Gloria Nemerowicz
Library Research:
Jill Kasen   Albert Record
Michael Pinchak
Interviewing:
Kathy Kenyon   Kenneth Robertson
Coding:
Claire McCartney

Interviewing and Coding:

Barbra Apfelbaum

Helena Goldstein

Meyer Goldstein

Barbara Howley

Michael Kissida

Jeanne Landry

Marsha Lichtenstein

Edward Martinez

Robert Phillips

Yolanda Prieto

Judith Rotter

Roseann Stevenson

Paula Taubman

Arthur Thompson

Henry Walentowicz

Interviewing, Coding, and Analysis:

Mary Goldstein

Emily Kaplan

Library Research, Interviewing, and Coding:

Mark Anderson

Arthur DeGrandis

Liaison for Computer Work:

William Dolphin

Typing:

Roberta Corrette

Keypunching:

Barbara Blocker

Debra Brenner

Eileen Scardino

Dr. Elaine W. House, Rutgers University, contributed her encouragement, her assistance in making contact with school systems, and her interest in the topic under study. Dr. Coralie Farlee, then at Rutgers, was instrumental in the development of the research proposal that lead to the funding of the work. And since we were funded, an input without which the study could not have been done, we express our appreciation to the Division of Vocational Education, New Jersey State Department of Education, and particularly to Dr. Morton Margules who, as Associate State Director of Vocational-Technical Education, encouraged and supported the research.

CHILDREN AND WORK

Chapter 1

Origins, Foci, and Procedures

"By the time a human being has reached the age of four or five," writes Peter Drucker, "he has been conditioned to work. To be sure, child labor is outlawed in most countries, but learning the fundamentals of being a person . . . creates the habit of work . . . Work is an extension of personality. It is achievement. It is one of the ways in which a person defines himself or herself, measures his worth and his humanity."[1]

Along with marriage, the family, education, and politics, work is one of our most basic and pervasive cultural institutions. Like so many other things taken for granted, work-related perceptions, beliefs and values are acquired gradually through the learning process. This volume will study such occupational socialization during childhood, focusing upon the development of work orientations among elementary school children.

Three Sources of Concern With Socialization to Work

The investigation of children's work orientations necessarily becomes an interdisciplinary effort, since the topic lies at the nexus of three intellectual traditions. The first is the long-standing sociological interest in the meaning of work and its place in human society. Closely related is another approach concerned primarily with learning, with charting the course of human growth during the process of socialization. Finally, there is an applied or pragmatic tradition upheld by educators and counselors professionally involved in the development and implementation of policy with respect to career education. To establish the context in which the present investigation originated, it is important to briefly examine each of these three contributing schools of thought.

Sociological Perspective on Work

To refer to *the* sociological perspective on work is to invite argument, for anyone with even a casual acquaintance with the field can identify numerous areas of sociological concern with work. Social scientists have long been interested in the social functions of work for the individual and for society. They have examined the linkages between work and the social structure in studies of occupational inheritance, the allocation of work roles, and the relationships between work roles and life style. They have explored the social-psychological dimensions of work, notably the occupational self-identity, dual cultural definitions of work as curse and blessing, and work-related alienation. And they have focused considerable attention on the behavior of the worker and of work groups, including such phenomena as the recruitment and training of members of occupational groups, their passage through careers, and patterns of social mobility associated with such careers.

To appreciate the underlying continuity in the sociology of work, one must trace the tradition back at least to Max Weber's classic treatise, *The Protestant Ethic and the Spirit of Capitalism.*[2] Among other things, Weber presented perhaps the first analysis of work orientations at the cultural level. The Protestant ethic was above all else a *work* ethic, a peculiar evaluation of the importance and dignity of human labor. At this point in our study the fact that Weber went beyond this in his fascination with the interpenetration of religious and secular value systems is a peripheral matter. What is crucial here is that, in introducing the study of work, he raised an important sociological question which has prompted our continued concern with work: What is the *significance* of work in human society?

Recent years have witnessed increased public concern with the fate of the worker and, indeed, of working. From Studs Terkel to Richard Nixon, in newspaper series and in the reports of presidential commissions, the message is clear: Work in our time is viewed as problematic in many respects.

Peter Berger, a contemporary sociologist who has not lost sight of the lessons of Weber, considers "the problem of work" to be a peculiarly modern one, a problem of meaning.[3] Meaning, he reminds us, is not ordinarily problematic; rather, it becomes so as transformations in the social order cause questions to be raised with regard to "previously taken-for-granted institutionalizations and legitimations."

Specifically, Berger points to two threats to the stability of the social meaning of work. The first has to do with structural change in the form of a greatly intensified division of labor resulting in "fragmentation of specific work processes, removing the worker further and further from the product of his work." Under conditions of rapid technological and organizational change, occupational roles become more precarious than in traditional societies, and individuals accordingly find difficulty in establishing and maintaining occupational self-identities. To Berger the contemporary shift in the search for identity to the "private sphere" and the "wild scramble" for occupational status (as seen in escalating efforts to "professionalize" numerous occupations) represent people's efforts to cope with the diminution of the meaning of work.

The second problem area with respect to the meaning of work in contemporary life involves, according to Berger, a true paradox. As Weber had shown, there is an ideological dimension to work. Although the work ethic has gradually been secularized, it has persisted "maximally in the expectation that work will provide the ultimate 'fulfillment' of the individual's life, and minimally in the expectation that in some shape or form, work will have some meaning for him personally." This secularized concept of vocation has become institutionalized; it finds support in our educational system and elsewhere. And yet the changes in the social organization of work make it less likely that one will find the gratification that has come to be culturally expected of work. Thus, the major questions in the sociology of work—structural, ideological, or otherwise—are ultimately related to the more basic question of the significance of the social institution of work in human life.

The present study reflects this tradition. That is to say, the investigation of orientations to work among children is primarily an effort to explore the social definitions of work and various work-related phenomena held during the elementary school years. A major goal of the project is to capture the "child's eye" view of the world of work.

Given the pervasiveness of work and its importance as a source of both identity and life satisfaction, it is important to examine children's early relationships with this social institution. It will also be of interest to note the extent to which ascriptive factors—age, sex, socio-economic status—are associated with variations in children's work orientations. The present study was undertaken for purposes of examining just such questions.

Socialization Theory

Occupational psychologist Henry Borow, in referring to the child or adolescent as the "worker to be," has alluded to the importance of another area of inquiry by social scientists.[4] The child does not start out as a worker—rather, he or she is transformed into one. This transformation, from the standpoint of the individual, is a learning process. From the standpoint of the society, it is a process of socialization.

In any society, the continuity and stability of social institutions depend upon the effectiveness with which members pass on relevant knowledge, skills, and value systems to their successors. So it is with work. "Socialization to the world of work," according to Wilbert E. Moore, involves "both cognitive learning and at least minimal internalization of appropriate norms."[5]

While there is nothing inherent in this definition of occupational socialization that should make it so, students of this learning process have largely concentrated their attention on the events of adolescence and early adulthood: career choice, occupational recruitment and training, and the acquisition of specific work group norms. Such tendencies are understandable insofar as these are the most visible benchmarks in the transformation of the nonworker into the mature occupant of an occupational role. And these are the phenomena which have the most direct bearing on subsequent success and career satisfaction.

It is important, however, to bear in mind that choices, for example, are extremely complex matters. To choose is to weigh and establish priorities among alternatives. This is not to imply that choice behavior is necessarily conducted on a rational or even conscious plane, or that it is not subject to all manner of psychosocial and situational restrictions. But the impact of one's experiences and the opportunity structure notwithstanding, clearly the "chooser" must have at his or her command a pool of information about the world of work and related values and attitudes. Such a behavioral repertoire does not appear from the void as the matter of one's occupational choice becomes imminent. Rather, it is developed gradually and in subtle fashion over most of a lifetime with the aid of a variety of socializing agents to whom the child is entrusted and/or exposed.

The lessons of socialization theory in general, and of developmental psychology in particular, dictate that childhood experiences be taken into account in any effort to understand later behavior. That the prominent theorists of occupational socialization (with the notable exceptions of Ginzberg and Roe) have emphasized later stages of the learning process does not lessen the need to explore the earlier development of the cognitive and evaluative "groundwork" upon which later work-related behavior is ultimately based. This study was conceived as such an effort.

In any study of socialization, one must take care to identify which elements of the process will be under examination. In this case, the primary emphasis will be upon *content,* i.e., upon what the child's work-related perceptions, attitudes, and values are. Much attention will also be paid to *processual factors,* in particular to age-related changes in children's work orientations.

The Career Education Perspective

While social scientists ordinarily confine their efforts to describing the social order, others shoulder the burden of tinkering with it. It is in this light that the career education movement must be viewed.

In a culture which has tended since the turn of this century to rely to an increasing degree upon formal organizations for the socialization of its youth, it is not surprising that pressure should be brought upon the educational establishment to improve the fit between curricular programs and the real world which students entered upon leaving school. As early as 1910, the American Federation of Labor and National Association of Manufacturers became strong, if unlikely, allies in a lobbying effort directed at the introduction of vocational instruction to the public school curriculum.[6] Elsewhere, there were other signs of awakening awareness of the importance of vocationally relevant education. In 1911, for example, Harvard offered the first university course in vocational guidance. Two years later the National Vocational Guidance Association was founded.[7] The 1917 passage of the Smith-Hughes Act put the federal government in the business of supporting vocational education.[8]

Intervening years have witnessed the growth and continuation of the movement. Earlier concerns with direct instruction in specific work skills and with vocational guidance in the clinical sense now share the spotlight with efforts to routinize the presentation of occupational information to an enlarged target population. With time has come the recognition, as anthropologist James Spradley put it, that "in our complex, rapidly-changing society, the necessary information about career opportunities cannot be gained during the senior year in high school. It must be imported throughout the course of one's education, from beginning to end."[9]

The contemporary career education movement has as its primary goal the enabling of informed occupational decision making on the part of the individual. The federal government and the states have made serious commitments to the achievement of this goal, starting with a $42.1 million research and development program in fiscal 1972. The Vocational Education Act of 1973 and subsequent legislation have provided the administrative apparatus and financial impetus for state level programs of major proportions.

Career education was hailed at its arrival by the United States Commissioner of Education Sidney P. Marland as "an idea whose time has come" and "the single largest initiative toward educational change" in this country.[10] Whether it fulfills such expectations will depend upon many things, not the least of which is the soundness of the informational base in which it is grounded. As Spradley has observed, success will require bringing students information of three sorts: (1) about their own aptitudes and interests; (2) about the "specifications" for a range of occupations, i.e., job prerequisites, opportunities, pay scales, etc.; and (3) about the "occupational cultures"—lifestyles, values, and assumptions—associated with membership in occupational groups.[11]

It is truism of developmental psychology that not all information is capable of being grasped or appreciated by children at every age level. Thus, given the substantial investment of human and financial resources in career education programs, care must be taken to present world-of-work information to children (1) at times when they are likely to understand it, and (2) before they have learned it "on their own," correctly or otherwise. The latter condition is included in recognition of the great costs to learning of boredom and in frank acknowledgement of the fact that disabusing children of their misconceptions is not something at which our schools have been demonstrably successful.

The present investigation seeks to establish baselines of information about children's orientations to work. While several previous investigations, many of which will be reported here, have explored various aspects of children's knowledge, attitudes, or behavior in relation to the world of work, there remained a need for a thorough, systematic, empirical investigation based upon the responses of a larger and more representative sample. It is hoped that the results of this study will prove beneficial to members of the educational community—from policymakers to classroom teachers—interested in the questions of when and how to present occupational information to children.

Work Orientations: Some Conceptual Clarifications

In 1972 the Brookings Institution published a study which critically examined evidence regarding the popular assumption that poor people stay on welfare out of dislike for work. The findings, in general, indicated that welfare recipients internalize the same positive norms and values that dominate our cultural orientations toward work. But unsatisfactory work experiences related to an extremely limited opportunity structure subsequently combine to erode these values.[12]

This study influenced the present investigation in two ways. First, it demonstrated that the nebulous phenomenon of "work orientations" could be systematically investigated. And, indirectly, it provided additional support for the position that children's work orientations merit further study, since it convincingly illustrated the manner in which such orientations affect subsequent work activity. The "action" or "feedback" model employed in the study posited that work orientations at Time 1 influence actions in the work situation at Time 2. The resulting experience reinforces or alters one's orientations at Time 3, which in turn influence action at Time 4, and so on. The significance of all this, for purposes of the present investigation, lies in the fact that the true "Time 1" may very well occur during childhood.

But precisely what are work orientations? While Goodwin's *Do the Poor Want to Work?* admirably illustrates the possibility of a systematic empirical study of work orientations, in terms of its operationalization of the concept it is not a good model for emulation here. To Goodwin, work orientations are "psychological attributes that significantly influence activity in the work world."[13] This is an "action model" in the true sense, since it explores the linkages between certain mental constructs and actual behavior. This approach works only if one has the luxury of access of objective data indicative of the actual working behavior of the research subjects.

Obviously, this is not a fruitful strategy when one's research subjects are children whose "work" ranges from the bare minimum of uncompensated household chores to regular part-time jobs for wages. Moreover, the fact that the present study is based upon children's self-reports of their work, rather than verifiable observations or records, is further reason to consider the Goodwin model inappropriate for use here.

A more fruitful approach is that of Smith and Proshansky, who define orientation to work as "a complex cognitive structure or system of beliefs relevant to the nature and consequences of socially defined task activities."[14] In other words, work orientations refer to one's *definition of the situation* with respect to work. Broadly interpreted, this may be taken to include beliefs, perceptions, attitudes, likes and dislikes, and values. At the risk of emphasizing the obvious, it is stressed that work orientations, while they may include occupational choice, extend beyond that.

Some examples of the various components of children's work orientations will clarify the sense in which the term is to be used in the present study. *Beliefs* and *perceptions* comprise an important part of one's orientation to the world of work. These are cognitive matters. There is no necessary correspondence between cognition and reality, i.e., erroneous beliefs and misconceptions may be just as important as accurate perceptions in the assessment of children's work orientations. For example, consider the child's impression of the process of getting a job. Some children are extremely sophisticated in their grasp of such matters, including in their accounts such things as aptitude test results, professional training, and even placement agencies. In contrast, there is the case of the boy who explained to the interviewer that one who wishes to become a doctor has only to hang out a shingle and begin helping sick people. Both versions, while vastly different in terms of their accuracy, represent important pieces of information about the child's view of the world of work.

Children also make evaluations about matters related to work. While they may not necessarily be able to articulate their *values*, they do seem to establish and rely upon priorities. This becomes especially obvious when children are asked to rank statements and/ or justify positions. This study examines, for example, children's abilities to rank a number of items in terms of their relative importance in thinking about one's career plans. It also looks into such matters as whether the child attaches a moral significance to working.

No effort to document the child's definition of work-related reality would be complete without including attitudinal factors. *Attitudes* are affective states that color perceptions, underpin evaluative judgments, and influence activities. This study will present evidence illustrating that children have a wide range of *feelings* about work. Moreover, such affective states, it will be shown, are inextricably linked to cognitive and evaluative aspects of work orientations. This is so not only because children act on the basis of their feelings, but also because during the egocentric years of childhood they generalize from the same basis, projecting their own feelings upon the rest of the world.

Not all of children's *experiences* with the world of work are vicarious or second-hand. Most children do in fact engage in activities which they, at least, consider to be "work." Very often they are paid for doing so. Thus, one must also take experiential factors into account in the analysis of children's work orientations. This is especially true in light of Goodwin's previously-mentioned findings about the strong reciprocal relationship between work orientations and actual job experiences. Thus, following the lead of psychologist Mary Engel, close attention will be paid to the phenomenon of "childwork."[15] There will be an examination of the jobs children have had, the nature of the compensation they have received, and the satisfactions or dissatisfactions derived from working.

These then are the principal components of work orientations in this study: cognitive factors (beliefs and perceptions), evaluative factors (values of priorities), affective factors (attitudes and feelings), and experiential factors (history of task performance).

Three Paths to Follow

Three models contributed in important ways to the conceptual framework of this project. Economist Eli Ginzberg and his associates pioneered in the investigation of behavior *leading up to* occupational choice, although their interests primarily centered on the latter. This necessarily alerted those who followed to the importance of childhood experiences in the process of growing into one's place in the working world. From the research of several political scientists interested in the political socialization of children came invaluable lessons with respect to the analysis of the *content* of the child's socialization experiences and, in particular, appropriate strategies for surveying youthful respondents. Finally, there are the "developmentalists" from various disciplines, who have in common a penchant for casting behavior in terms of growth or progress along a relatively typical temporal continuum. While Ginzberg suggested *what* to study and the political scientists showed *how* to do so, the developmentalists contributed insights into the interpretation of the *meaning* of findings. Each path merits further consideration.

Ginzberg Theory of Career Choice

As an economist concerned principally with the conservation of human resources, Ginzberg perceived a connection between the process of occupational choice and job satisfactions. As he put it, the individual "cannot make a choice without determining, at least preliminarily, what he wants to get out of work."[16] He recognized that occupational choice was a long-term process, the roots of which "can probably be found in the play activities of children." He set out to explore this process.

He began by sampling eleven-year-olds because this was the age at which it was felt that children had to begin to make some *slightly* vocationally relevant decisions. Selecting his respondents at two-year intervals, he assembled a cross-sectional sample extending from sixth grade to graduate school. The sample was admittedly not representative of the general population. Rather, it was deliberately composed of highly intelligent white males of Anglo-Saxon background, the children of upper middle class families in New York City. The rationale for this was to select respondents who theoretically had maximum freedom from restrictions in an effort to study the decision-making process in a relatively unencumbered population.

Ginzberg's findings, based upon eight interviews at each grade level sampled, were surprisingly far-reaching. His own summary, years later, was as follows:[17]

> Occupational choice, we said, is a decision-making *process* that extends from pre-puberty until the late teens or early 20's when the individual makes a definite occupational commitment. Many educational and other preparatory and exploratory decisions along the way have the quality of *irreversibility:* A student who is pursuing a pre-law curriculum cannot suddenly shift tack and seek admission to medical school, for example. Thirdly, the resolution of the choice process always ends in a compromise, since the individual seeks to find an optimal fit between his interests, capacities, and values and the world of work.

His subsequent reappraisal, twenty years after publication of the original theory, touched on all three of its elements. First of all, Ginzberg no longer considers the process limited to a decade, but open-ended in the sense that occupational decision-making can extend for one's entire working life. Second, while he still feels that one's decisions have a cumulative effect on one's occupational prospects, he no longer sees these as necessarily having an irreversible impact. Retraining, relocation, and promotional opportunities may enable the individual to nullify the effects of previous decisions. And, he prefers now to think of the process as one of *optimalization* rather than compromise, i.e., one of achieving the best fit between one's wishes and existing circumstances, not necessarily just settling for what one can.[18]

Ginzberg viewed the choice process as composed of three major stages: the fantasy period, the period of tentative choice, and the period of realistic choices. The first two of these, since they encompass children of ages six to eleven and eleven to seventeen, respectively, are directly relevant here.

Although Ginzberg did not actually include children throughout much of the so-called fantasy or latency period, he did discuss it. This is a time during which[19]

A child is free from all urgency to deal with his occupational choice in a concrete manner. He can choose any occupation and there are no limits to this fantasy. There is no bridge between the present and the future, so that he is under no pressure to figure out how to accomplish his goal.

The use of the term "fantasy" in characterizing the stage occupied by children six to eleven years old need not imply that children project themselves into any imaginary world of specific fanciful goals. They do not perceive the relationship between means and ends in thinking about their futures, and their thought processes in this respect are not yet rational or objective. Nor do they have to be so at this point. Consider again our earlier example of the child under the impression that hanging out a shingle enables one to practice medicine. In a child of, say, eight years of age it is hard to imagine any serious consequences for holding such a belief, if only because there is so little opportunity to act on the basis of it.

It is during this time that the child comes to recognize that he or she will one day have to work. "Not to work is inconceivable to them!" writes Ginzberg of the children in this age bracket.[20] Gradually, during the preadolescent years, the child becomes critical of earlier fantasy choices. As one's outlook broadens and becomes more realistic, previous wishes to become a cowboy or film star tend to be seen as "kid's stuff." The child, possibly beginning to feel pressures from parents and teachers to develop good working habits, also senses the approach of a "right age" for the making of work-related choices.

The *tentative period,* ages eleven through seventeen, is divided by Ginzberg into four substages: the interest, capacity, value, and transition stages. The first two, since they encompass the years from eleven to fourteen, are the ones which concern us here.

The *interest stage* (ages eleven to twelve) follows the child's recognition that he or she personally must make an occupational choice. The first tentative steps in that direction are formulated on the basis of sources of satisfaction to the child, namely "likes" and "dislikes." Children of this age group recognize that their intentions might shift. But such changes, they feel, will nevertheless be rooted in their interests, i.e., they will occur because the children grow to like something else or no longer like a previous choice as much.

It is only slightly later, during the *capacity stage* (typically ages thirteen to fourteen), that children also begin to take their own abilities into account. "I'm good at X, so I'll consider being a ——." "I'm not very good at Y, so I couldn't be a ——, *no matter how much I might like to be.*" These are the sorts of statements one is more likely to hear from a young adolescent than a child of eight or nine. They are indicative of a qualitative change in the direction of increased vocational maturity.

The remaining substages of the tentative period refer to the high school years and need not directly concern us here. The third period described by Ginzberg, the era of realism, has to do with the final aspects of settling upon a choice: further training or education, if relevant, and job experiences leading directly or indirectly to entry into a career track.

The work of Ginzberg and associates is important in several respects. First, it sensitized researchers who followed to the utility of viewing the matter of occupational choice as a long-term process, each step of which, though it does not necessarily foreclose later options, certainly alters the probabilities associated with them. Moreover, it highlighted the significance of the childhood years in relation to subsequent occupational choices and work satisfactions. And whereas the theory ostensibly deals with occupational choice, it in fact addresses a more general issue, namely the broader question of the individual's introduction to the world of work. Without such a model, it is doubtful that the present investigation could or would have been undertaken.

Paradigms of Political Socialization

In the aftermath of Watergate, as if to prove that every cloud does indeed have a silver lining, politicians and news media personalities point to the stability that characterized the nation's political climate during that very difficult constitutional crisis. Political stability, as Herbert Hyman has observed, rests upon the fact that political behavior is *learned* behavior, i.e., a product of the process of socialization.[21] In recent years political scientists have devoted considerable attention to socialization to politics during childhood. Their work has been instructive in several respects.

Fred Greenstein laid down a simple set of ground rules for framing research questions regarding *any* kind of socialization. The complete analytical picture, he stated, could be obtained by answering the five-part question: (1) Who (2) learns what (3) from whom (4) under what conditions (5) with what consequences for behavior?[22] The political scientists, it is suggested, have been most active in pursuit of the second component of the formula, namely the investigation of the *content* of the child's socialization experiences. This political socialization model, with its stress upon the content of the learning process, is immensely helpful.

One of the earliest students of political socialization was psychologist Jean Piaget, who traced the development of the concept of "homeland" in two hundred Swiss children from four to fifteen years of age.[23] Hyman's theoretical writings on the general subject a few years later may have given impetus to the trend toward further investigation.[24] Since then, numerous studies have appeared concerning children's awareness of law and legal and political authority figures; their knowledge of political institutions, such as political parties or the branches of government; the internalization of ideological positions, such as the norms regarding patriotism, duty, freedom and participation; and the onset of partisanship.[25] As a result of such activity there now exists a well-documented body of literature addressed to what children know of the world of politics, and the age at which they typically know it.

Another important outcome of the research of these political scientists is improved knowledge of the timing of the growth of children's awareness of politics. As Hess and Torney put it: "The most striking feature of political socialization in the elementary school is the extent to which basic orientations have been acquired by children by the end of the eighth grade."[26] While they found that progress was rapid, it was by no means uniform. Grades three through five seem especially important in terms of the acquisition of attitudes.

Greenstein concurred, choosing to study children ages nine to thirteen out of a conviction that this was[27]

> an undramatic but crucial period of both social-psychological and political development . . . since during this time . . . children move from near—but not complete—ignorance of adult politics to awareness of most of the conspicuous features of the adult political arena.

After reviewing the existing research on the development of politcal behavior, Hyman concluded: "The beginnings of participation must be sought in relatively early childhood years, for already, by age sixteen, the phenomenon seems to be well-informed, not very disparate from the adult level manifested by the group in their twenties."[28]

In the face of such consensus, anyone concerned with parallels between the development of political orientations and that of work orientations must be cognizant of the need to include in the study children of even the earliest years of elementary school.

But to include such young children saddles the researcher with additional problems, for social scientists are typically unaccustomed to surveying respondents whose verbal skills, cognitive styles, and vocabularies are so different from those of adults. At a later point, attention will be devoted to the explanation of the development of strategies and techniques for obtaining usable information from children.

Developmentalist Approach

Earlier, in considering socialization theory, reference was made to the "developmentalists." It is now time to clarify the relationship between socialization theory and what is here termed *developmentalism*.

Socialization refers broadly to the process by which new members are brought into social groups and equipped with that which they will need to function smoothly within them—information, norms, attitudes, etc. Whether one thinks of this as benign guidance or as a group's exercise of power over an individual, it is clear that the process has at least the following characteristics:

1. It is *interactive,* i.e., it involves the actions, reactions, and reinforcements of persons other than the one being socialized.
2. It is directed at the *conferring of an identity* of some sort.
3. It involves *role learning,* the imparting of a range of mutual expectations associated with performance of one or more social roles.
4. It is intrinsically *connected with social control,* since it provides the basis for predictability within the group and is the vehicle through which both positive and negative sanctions are made meaningful to group members.

Developmentalism, for our purposes, refers to a particular approach to socialization which emphasizes, in the words of Donald Super, "the progressive increase and modification of the individual's behavioral repertoire through growth and learning . . . marked by sequential stages of increasing competence."[29] Theorists in this group stress regular, cumulative aspects of the growth process. They seek, for example, to establish the existence of basic age-related patterns and to chart the learning curves typically associated with growth into various awarenesses. Theirs is a normative approach; it is over-whelming concerned with ascertaining what the growth norms are and the conditions under which variations occur. The child's *readiness* to perceive, to do, or to feel certain things is often a focal point of studies in this tradition.

We will examine contributions of a few of the better-known developmentalists whose works are deemed relevant for interpretation of the findings presented in later chapters. The theories of Piaget, Erikson, Havighurst, and Super will be discussed briefly in that order. It should be noted that psychologist Anne Roe occupies a prominent position among developmental theorists. Her major interests, however, center on the relationship between personality factors and occupational interests during adolescence and beyond.[30] Her work is not considered directly relevant to the present investigation and, accordingly, will not be discussed here.

Piaget

Swiss psychologist Jean Piaget has devoted his lengthy career to the study of child development. Any attempt to render a capsule summary of his work would be futile. Instead, let us merely point to those of his ideas which influenced the framing of questions in the present study.[31]

To Piaget, all intellectual development is to be understood in terms of *adaptation* to one's environment. Adaptation consists of two processes: assimilation ("taking in" that which one experiences, making it one's own) and accommodation (adjusting to the environment). The developmental process involves the constant search for *equilibrium* between what the child understands and the remainder of his/her experiences with the environment. The child's struggle to balance the two never ceases, since equilibrium is a transitory state. Once reached, it is constantly upset and must be resought at a higher plane.

Such a view of development implies that special attention must be paid to the child's *readiness* to grasp certain concepts. To Piaget, it is "pedagogical mania" for adults to attempt to accelerate children's learning without also increasing the range of experiences available to them. Such an observation is important in relation to the introduction of career education materials to the elementary curriculum, for it implies that such efforts may in many instances be undertaken in vain. One of the primary motivations for studying children's work orientations involves the desire to know which work-related concepts children typically understand at certain points in their development. (This is not to be confused with a projection of what children *might be capable of understanding,* given certain increments in their experiences with their environment.)

Another of Piaget's contributions is his *theory of stages.* He divides development from birth to adulthood into four generic periods (each of which is subdivided into several stages). The important thing, he reminds us, is not the chronological age at which the child passes through each—for the pace may vary—but the sequence, which remains constant.

The first and second periods refer to development ordinarily completed by about the time of the child's entry into the elementary school. These would be of little consequence here except that in describing them Piaget stressed the importance of play and imitation to the child's assimilation and accommodation efforts, respectively. Such thinking sheds considerable light on the significance of the child's playing at such roles as doctor and teacher. This "ludic symbolism," as Piaget calls children's "make believe" games, is critical in bridging the developmental gap between the egocentric world of the toddler and the adult world.

The third period in Piaget's developmental schema is that of *concrete operations.* It extends roughly from the seventh through the eleventh years. As language skills develop, the child's facility for mental operations increases in sophistication. Of particular interest here is the fact that children of this age group, while typically still incapable of truly abstract thinking, develop the capacity for *logically grouping* the objects they encounter. Should this apply to tangible social objects—specifically, to workers—it would present the opportunity to test for the salient dimensions of children's perceptions of the world of work. This could be done by asking children to construct categories from a list of workers and to label or describe same. According to Piaget, children might be expected to do so by "class inclusion" (combining objects within broader categories) and by employing the "logic of relations" (specifying the relationships perceived between objects). Children's behavior was examined in this regard.

Children beyond the age of eleven ordinarily enter what Piaget calls the *period of formal operations*. Abstract thinking emerges at this point, manifesting itself in concern with the discovery and application of general principles behind specific instances. It will be of interest, therefore, to note the extent to which the responses of seventh graders differ qualitatively from those of younger children in the study. This should be especially visible in cases in which children are given the opportunity to furnish explanations and value judgments with respect to work-related stimuli. (Unfortunately, as will become apparent, several circumstances limited our abilities to gather information from seventh graders. The costs of such limitations in terms of the quality and comparability of data were in some cases substantial.)

Although he was not directly concerned with the child's experiences with the world of work, per se, Piaget has provided many valuable insights into the interpretation of age-related differences in children's responses in general. The present study, while not intended to *test* Piaget's theories, will rely heavily upon them in assigning meaning to observed age differences in children's work orientations.

Erikson

Erik Erikson's bent, although much more psychoanalytic than that of Piaget, is no less developmental. In a manner reminiscent of Freud's portrayal of psychosexual stages, Erikson posits a series of *psychosocial stages* through which the developing child passes. Like Piaget, he emphasizes sequence rather than chronology. To him, each stage represents a "decisive encounter" between child and environment, the outcome of which is ideally an increased understanding or conceptual growth. Each stage may be viewed in the abstract as a struggle between two antithetical traits. For example, the infant's first hurdle is to achieve a "favorable ratio" of "basic trust" over "basic mistrust" in its relationships with parents.[32]

Erikson speaks of eight psychosocial stages, three of which are relevant to the development of children's work orientations. Although he does not specify the ages typically associated with each stage, it is clear that the third, fourth, and fifth stages typically encompass roughly the years five through fifteen.

The third of the eight stages is the so-called *locomotorgenital* period. During this time, the child develops initiative, "the quality of undertaking, planning, and 'attacking' a task for the sake of being active and on the move . . ." The child "can gradually develop a sense of moral responsibility . . . gain insights into the institutions, functions, and roles which permit his responsible participation . . . find pleasurable accomplishment in wielding tools and weapons, in manipulating toys, and in caring for younger children."[33]

Following such cues, we asked even our youngest respondents about the nature of their chores and whether they take pleasure in them, etc. For it is during the early years of elementary school, according to Erikson, that the roots of the child's "work-identification" and internalization of an "economic ethos" must be sought.[34]

This period is followed by the *latency stage,* during which the child "must begin to be a worker and potential provider." The child of ten will ideally overcome feelings of inferiority while at the same time developing a *"sense of industry*—i.e., he adjusts himself to the inorganic laws of the tool world. He can become an eager and absorbed unit of a productive situation. To bring a productive situation to completion—supercedes the whims and wishes of play." The child of this age internalizes the *work principle,* or comes to appreciate work completion and diligence. Simultaneously, the technological ethos of the culture is imparted: The child becomes accustomed to handling utensils and tools and develops a "sense of division of labor and of differential opportunity."[35] Clearly, Erikson's account of this fourth developmental stage offers a wealth of suggestions about what to look for among our respondents.

Only a relatively small proportion of pupils in the study will have reached Erikson's fifth stage, *puberty/adolescence.* Childhood ends and youth begins, Erikson says, when one has established "a good initial relationship to the world of skills and tools, and with the advent of puberty." The most important changes during youth involve the development of an *identity*. The adolescent must integrate interests, aptitudes, and opportunities to play social roles in the resolution of who he or she is. The greatest threat to identity, he reminds us, is role confusion, since it engenders within the individual doubts with respect to identity.

Youth is also a time for the emergence of introspection. The crises faced by adolescents involve the reconciliation of disparities between "what they appear to be in the eyes of others as compared to what they feel they are." It is also a time for concern with "how to connect the roles and skills cultivated earlier with the occupational prototypes of the day . . . They are ever-ready to install lasting idols and ideals as guardians of a final identity."[36] Erikson is in effect alluding here to the importance of *role models* in the emergence of work orientations. This is a caveat which will be taken most seriously in this study.

Havighurst

Robert Havighurst, unlike Piaget and Erikson, has been interested in the developmental process specifically as it relates to work. Moreover, his emphasis has not been restricted to changes in work orientations from childhood through the early adult years. Rather, he conceives of vocational development as a life-long process divisible into six stages. The first two are relevant here, since they include children from five to fifteen. The third stage also bears mentioning, since some respondents are probably already engaged in the developmental tasks which typify it.

The first stage in Havighurst's account of vocational development is that of *identification with a worker*. It includes children in the general vicinity of five to ten years of age. During this period, the child's identification with parents and other significant persons ordinarily assures that "the concept of working becomes an essential part of the ego ideal."[37] The child of this age group has several developmental tasks: (1) the development of fundamental skills in reading, writing, and calculating; (2) learning the physical skills necessary for games; (3) learning to get along with age-mates; (4) learning appropriate sex roles; (5) developing the concepts necessary for daily life; (6) developing conscience, a sense of morality, and values; and (7) achieving personal independence. Havighurst is extremely confident of the efficacy of basing predictions of future career directions upon the performance of children *by the age of ten*.[38]

For children in the ten-to-fifteen-year-old bracket, the focus shifts to *acquiring the basic habits of industry*. By this it is meant that the child must learn to do schoolwork and chores and to effectively allocate time and energy. One learns the conditions under which it is appropriate to put work before play.

All of this leads up to the third stage in the process, that of *acquiring identity as a worker in the occupational structure.* During adolescence and early adulthood one prepares for work, gets valuable work experience, and develops a basis for both the making of an occupational choice and the assumption of economic independence in a family of one's own. Clearly, Havighurst considers the process to be cumulative, i.e., the visible changes of this period definitely rest upon the more subtle aspects of prior growth.

The assumption of an *occupational identity* is the culmination of a whole range of previous socializing experiences. But it does not mark the end of growth. That Havighurst sees the process of vocational development extending through, and even beyond, one's working years is important here insofar as it posits a connection between childhood development and work satisfaction throughout one's lifetime. This highlights the importance of gaining additional insight into children's socialization into the world of work.

Super

Occupational psychologist Donald Super has presented a theory of vocational development which integrates the work of Ginzberg and others[39] while relying heavily upon the notion of developmental tasks put forward by Havighurst. He, too, saw the process as life-long. He traced it through five stages to a period called *decline,* consisting of career "deceleration" and retirement.[40]

For our purposes, only the first or *growth* stage (birth to age fourteen) is relevant. "Self concept," Super writes of this period, "develops through identification with key figures in family and in school; needs and fantasy are dormant early in this stage; interest and capacity becomes more important in this stage with increasing social participation and reality-testing."[41]

If this sounds reminiscent of Ginzberg's theory, it is intentionally so. Following Ginzberg, Super subdivides the growth stage into the "fantasy," "interest," and "capacity" sub-stages. During the fantasy period (ages four through ten), role playing is extremely important. Later, during brief periods of interests (ages eleven and twelve), the child's "likes" and "dislikes" come to the forefront and serves as major determinants of aspirations and activities. Then, about the age of thirteen, the child begins to take his/her abilities into account, and to weigh job requirements in thinking of future career directions. This is the capacity stage.

Super's theory is couched almost entirely in terms of what he calls *vocational maturity*. That is to say, he measures development largely in terms of how "mature" the behavior is in relation to that of one's age peers. But he urges the application of a two-dimensional standard of vocational maturity which takes into account both chronological age norms and the individual's performance of developmental tasks, regardless of whether they are confronted at the appropriate age.

As yardsticks for the assessment of maturity, Super has listed the "vocational developmental tasks" considered appropriate at different life stages.[42] The elementary school child, he notes, must master the abilities: (1) to undertake cooperative enterprises; (2) to choose activities which suit individual abilities; (3) to assume responsibility for one's actions; and (4) to perform household chores.

These, then, are the developmentalists whose works have contributed to the perspective of the present investigation. Those works surveyed convey the key message of the developmentalist tradition, namely that behavioral changes over time in the maturing individual are best understood in the context of regular and meaningful patterns of growth. While the present investigation is not intended to test prominent developmental theories, it does acknowledge a great debt to them. For in addition to suggesting the nature of questions which might be asked of children, the works of the developmentalists have served as valuable guideposts in the interpretation of findings.

Research Procedures

Decisions concerning research design, the selection of the principal variables, research instruments, and data collection procedures depend upon both the nature of the questions being asked and practical considerations (such as attributes of the research site and sample population and financial and temporal restrictions). This being an exploratory study, the primary research goals were descriptive: to ascertain patterns in children's increasing involvement with the world of work; to document the salient aspects of work and working in their eyes; and to inquire into the nature of systematic differences in children's work orientations.

The ideal strategy for a developmental study is a longitudinal design. One does not always have the luxury, however, of conducting the ideal study. Given the limitations of time and financial support, a cross-sectional design was employed as a next-best approximation of the longitudinal approach. In keeping with procedures followed in other studies of childhood socialization, pupils in grades one, three, five and seven were sampled.

Respondents attended schools in five communities in north central New Jersey. The cooperating schools had in common that they were suburban or semi-rural in location and overwhelmingly white in enrollment. (Data collected from a sixth community at an inner-city school whose pupils were almost exclusively black or Puerto Rican have been excluded from the analysis for methodological and ethical reasons.)[43] Thus, the sample was comprised largely of white suburban or exurban residents ranging in socioeconomic background from working class to upper-middle class. Generalizations must be limited accordingly, but the findings are thought to be representative of the largely white public primary school population of the state.

While no town is completely homogeneous in socioeconomic composition, the communities from which the pupils in this study were selected can be characterized as working-, middle-, and upper-middle class, respectively. "Jones Ferry" and "Spruce Creek" are venerable towns whose white frame homes and congenial business districts attest to the prosperity of times gone by. Both are classified for census purposes as "rural centers" but their inhabitants today typically earn their livings as non-farm industrial, retail, or clerical workers, or as shopkeepers. "Lincoln" and "Johnson Heights" are burgeoning middle-class bedroom communities whose occupants are a mixed lot of upwardly-mobile workers: skilled craftsmen and foremen, teachers and lower echelon bureaucrats, and a minority of junior executives and young professionals for whom these towns are "first stops" rather than long-term homes. "Exeter" is also a newer bedroom community populated not by "old wealth" but by upwardly-mobile business and professional persons, many of whom presumably regard themselves as having "arrived."

Table 1.1 depicts the distribution of male and female children in the sample, respectively, by grade in school and community of residence. Altogether, 905 children were surveyed. The reader will note that the numerical distribution by sex is weighted in favor of boys, who compromise 55 percent of the sample. Also, given the small number of cases in several cells of the Jones Ferry and Spruce Creek subsamples, it is necessary to collapse these into a single "rural center" category. Finally, the responses of seventh graders from the Johnson Heights school district are excluded from the analysis since, in the estimation of the research staff, extenuating circumstances rendered these data unsuitable for comparison with the responses of other seventh graders in the sample.[44]

TABLE 1.1
Distribution of males and females surveyed
by grade in school

MALES

	Grade in school				
Community:	1st	3rd	5th	7th	
Exeter	33	36	30	32	(131)
Johnson Heights	21	28	26	--*	(75)
Lincoln	65	66	49	26	(206)
Spruce Creek	11	3	6	12	(32)
Jones Ferry	18	12	7	15	(52)
	(148)	(145)	(118)	(85)	(496)

FEMALES

	Grade in school				
Community:	1st	3rd	5th	7th	
Exeter	26	23	29	29	(107)
Johnson Heights	26	20	31	--*	(77)
Lincoln	34	45	54	22	(155)
Spruce Creek	8	6	6	6	(26)
Jones Ferry	6	18	11	9	(44)
	(100)	(112)	(131)	(66)	(409)

*Johnson Heights seventh grade responses not usable.

Table 1.2 shows the general distribution by father's occupational status of children in each community. This table is based upon the

reports of those children (N-652) who furnished sufficient information to permit coding of father's occupation with some degree of
confidence. While there are considerable variations between communities, the overall sample is divided approximately evenly
between children of white- and blue-collar backgrounds. More specifically, 22 percent of these respondents are the children of profes-
sional/managerial workers, 31 percent are from other white-collar
backgrounds, and 47 percent come from blue-collar households.

TABLE 1.2
Children's reports of father's occupation
by community of residence*

Reported Occupational Status:	Rural	Johnson Heights	Exeter	Lincoln	Totals
Professional/ Managerial	12.7% (15)	25.5% (28)	43.3% (77)	8.5% (21)	21.6% (141)
Other White-collar	15.3 (18)	24.5 (27)	43.8 (78)	32.9 (81)	31.3 (204)
Blue-collar	72.0 (85)	50.0 (55)	12.9 (23)	58.5 (144)	47.1 (307)
Total cases:	118	110	178	246	652

*Percentages based upon the number of pupils in each com-
munity giving sufficiently clear reports to enable father's
occupation to be coded with some degree of confidence.

Data collection involving children, especially if it occurs on-site in
their schools, presents the researcher with many problems. Children's verbal skills and attention spans must be estimated in con-
structing research instruments and planning field work procedures.
Care must be taken to establish rapport between children and the
research team, while at the same time the inevitable impact of the
researchers' presence must be minimized. In recognition of such
problems, the first or "pilot" year of the project was set aside for
developing, pre-testing, and revising a battery of data collection
techniques appropriate for use across the grade levels sampled. Also,
considerable attention was devoted to evolving and testing strategies

to "normalize" the presence of the research team in the eyes of the children. With the cooperation of school personnel care was taken to identify members of the research team as "regulars" with whom children expected to routinely interact over a period of five to eight weeks.

Children were surveyed an average of from four to seven times during the course of the school site visits. As a general rule, first and third grade children either responded in groups to pictorial or simple verbal stimuli or were interviewed individually. Fifth and seventh graders ordinarily responded in writing to questionnaires or other verbal tasks.

It was necessary to develop a series of research instruments of varying formats developmentally appropriate for children of different age groups. As in any investigation of awareness of a culturally pervasive phenomenon, getting respondents to make explicit a variety of unstated work-related assumptions and taken-for-granted information was often problematic. Following numerous leads in the literature, and after considerable experimentation with replications and instruments of our own design, a battery of ten instruments (some of which had multiple versions) was finally adapted. These ranged in format from straightforward questionnaires about the world of work or parental work roles, to inquiries from a hypothetical "Man from Mars"[45] seeking explanations of everyday work-related phenomena, to picture-stimuli and drawing exercises, to tasks involving the sorting of occupations into categories, to the ranking of occupational value statements. While limitations of space necessarily prohibit detailed discussion and presentation of the actual instruments, the interested reader may obtain these elsewhere.[46]

The principal independent variable in any developmental study is of course age. This variable was operationalized in terms of grade in school, in keeping with standard practice in the educational and developmental literature. Thus, the first order of business in subsequent data chapters will ordinarily be documentation of age-related changes in children's work orientations. While no attempt has been made to establish a "gradient" or age-specific inventory of children's conceptual awareness, it is likely that some readers may wish to interpret the data in that context.

Sex, along with age, has traditionally served as a basis for the division of labor in most societies, including our own. Thus it is important to note the impact of sex differences upon children's developing work orientations. Put simply, in a society that has historically allocated work roles on the basis of gender, one must be alert for the obvious possibility that boys' and girls' work-related socializing experiences may differ accordingly. Moreover, since such a system of ascriptive role allocation has been the object of much criticism of late, one could hardly pass up the opportunity to explore the actual impact of sex differences upon children's work orientations in the 1970's. If, as is commonly believed, sex roles are indeed in transition, then it is of particular interest to examine such phenomena as sex-related differences in occupational interests and mobility aspirations, awareness of the world of work, and the sex-typing of workers and jobs. One wonders, of course, whether earlier research findings will appear "dated."

Social theorists have traditionally been concerned with the effects of position in the social structure upon numerous social-psychological attributes, including perceptions of "one's place" and of chances for improving one's lot. No investigation of socialization to work would be complete, therefore, without an examination of the relationships between *socioeconomic status* (SES) and children's work orientations.

While Borow[47] has suggested that the relation of SES to occupational preference among young children has not yet been clearly established, there are indications of the connections, in general, between social status and work orientations. Williams, for example, has observed that SES strongly influenced elementary school children's knowledge of certain monetary concepts, especially in the first grade. At all grade levels tested, she found the higher the socioeconomic status of the family, the greater the child's concept awareness tended to be.[48]

Smith and Proshansky viewed the issue largely in terms of class-related differentials in the child's acquired definitions of situations regarding the world of work. Fathers of different SES backgrounds may share with their families, if only inadvertently, markedly different attitudes toward work and job-related satisfactions. For example, in the middle class "getting ahead" implies mobility and promotion, whereas the same term in the lower class family may refer instead to achieving job security.[49] Lipsman has observed that poverty, in addition to placing economic or financial obstacles in the path of the individual, erects psychological or cultural barriers for the young. She interprets these within a Maslowian "need hierarchy" frame of reference, noting that while blue-collar children seek to satisfy their needs for security, middle class children, starting from positions of relative security, strive for esteem in their work experiences.[50]

Consider the following statement by Elkin in light of its obvious implications for a study of children's work orientations:[51]

> The upper middle class also places more emphasis on striving and achievement. The family, teachers, and even at times the peer group apply pressure on the child to study, seek good grades, strive for scholarship, and attain a respectable business or professional position ... This 'adaptive' or 'socialized' anxiety accompanies the development of a deferred gratification pattern. The child learns to postpone immediate gratifications for the rewards he might achieve in the future. If he worked hard at his studies, saves money, and avoids serious sexual entanglements, he might more easily attain a position which accords him wealth, prestige, and influence ... The lower class is preoccupied with the problems of immediate living ... The rewards offered by the middle class are too distant to be meaningful ... He is not stigmatized for failure in school or motivated to sacrifice for future gains. The teacher's words do not connect with the acts of training in his home.

Socioeconomic status is ordinarily measured in terms of occupation, education, or income. Since it was not feasible in this case to interview the parents of our respondents, it was necessary to base our estimates of SES upon the child's report of parental occupation, specifically that of the father.

It is clear that the use of second-hand information from young respondents whose knowledge of parental occupations may be incomplete or distorted entailed an unacceptable level of risk. A strategy was devised to proceed along more conservative lines in order to reduce the margin for error in the assessment of the child's SES. A two-fold procedure was employed in the classification of cases into High SES and Low SES subsamples. In the first place, all codable responses of children who furnished father's occupation were classified according to the seven occupational categories of the socioeconomic status index developed by August B. Hollingshead.[52] Thereafter, community of residence was also taken into account, since these communities were originally selected for their relative homogeneity on the SES dimension. This variable was used, in effect, as a check on the accuracy of the child's report. Low SES will be judged on the basis of the child's report of the father's occupation as working class (Hollingshead's occupational categories 5, 6, and 7) in those towns in which such backgrounds are quite common. High SES will be judged on the basis of the child's report of the father's occupation (Hollingshead's occupational categories 1 and 2) in predominantly middle class communities. Such a procedure, it is hoped, maximizes the "purity" of the High and Low SES subsamples respectively.

It had originally been intended to include in the analysis examination of the effects of two additional independent variables upon children's work orientations: intelligence and racial/ethnic identification. While both have been shown elsewhere to be potentially important factors in the socialization of the child, it has been impossible, given the constraints upon the nature and use of school records and the enormous variations in record-keeping procedures within the participating schools, to efficiently and reliably control for the effects of these two variables.

Four Focal Themes

The presentation of findings proceeds along thematic lines. Four major themes emerged which, taken together, convey the range of what is meant here by children's orientations to the world of work. Each of these themes is the subject of a separate chapter.

In chapter 2, children's basic knowledge of the world of work is examined. The concern here is with the determination of baselines of information and with the timing of cognitive development. We inquire broadly into *what* children know of the world of work and attempt to furnish some clues as to *when* they typically evidence such knowledge. Specifically, the focus is upon (1) children's grasps of basic economic and commercial relationships, (2) their recognition of the meaning of work and its place in social life, (3) their knowledge of selected work-related phenomena, (4) their own work and earning experiences, and (5) their occupational aspirations in light of the social positions of parental role models.

In chapter 3 the emphasis is upon evaluative aspects of children's work orientations. Specifically, there is an examination of whether elementary school children seem to have internalized the so-called Protestant ethic. We explore their attachment, or lack thereof, as the case may be, of moral significance to working and the importance of rewards in their views of the working world.

Chapter 4 deals with the early appearance of children's work-related feelings. Evidence is presented regarding children's various "likes" and "dislikes" with respect to work. And, the issue of children's "sex-typing" of occupations is explored, since it sheds light on the strength and nature of affective responses to the world of work.

Chapter 5 is concerned with children's awareness of social class and matters relating to socioeconomic differentiation. Social status is commonly employed, and rightly so, as a major independent variable in sociological studies of the socialization process. The implication, obviously, is that social scientists believe the world to be stratified in such a way that one's place within the system influences one's perceptions and experiences. But do children perceive the world in the same way? This is the subject of the chapter.

Finally, in chapter 6 the findings are summarized and discussed in light of their implications for educational policy.

Notes

1. Peter Drucker, *Management: Tasks, Responsibilities, Practices* (New York: Harper and Row, 1973), pp. 184-185.
2. Max Weber, *The Protestant Ethic and the Spirit of Capitalism,* trans. Talcott Parsons (New York: Charles Scribner's Sons, 1958).
3. Peter L. Berger, "Some General Observations on the Problem of Work," in *The Human Shape of Work,* ed. Peter L. Berger (New York: MacMillan and Co., 1964), pp. 211-241.
4. Henry Borow, "An Integral View of Occupational Theory and Research" in *Man in a World of Work,* ed. Henry Borow (Boston: Houghton-Mifflin, 1964), p. 364.
5. Wilbert E. Moore, "Occupational Socialization," in *Handbook of Socialization Theory and Research,* ed. David A. Goslin (Chicago: Rand McNally, 1969), p. 868.
6. Lawrence A. Cremin, *The Transformation of the School: Progressivism in American Education, 1876-1957* (New York: Random House, 1964), p. 50.
7. Henry Borow, "Milestones: A Chronology of Notable Events in the History of Vocational Guidance," in *Man in a World at Work,* ed. Henry Borow (Boston: Houghton-Mifflin Co., 1964), pp. 48-50.
8. Lawrence A. Cremin, *Transformation of the School,* pp. 56-57.
9. James P. Spradley, "Career Education in Cultural Perspective," in *Essays in Career Education,* ed. Larry McLure and Carolyn Buan (Portland, Ore.: Northwest Regional Educational Laboratory, 1973), p. 11.
10. Sidney P. Marland, "Forward," in *Essays on Career Education,* ed. Larry McClure and Carolyn Buan (Portland, Ore.: Northwest Regional Educational Laboratory, 1973), pp. vii-xi.
11. Spradley, "Career Education," pp. 11-12.
12. Leonard Goodwin, *Do the Poor Want to Work?: A Social-Psychological Study of Work Orientations* (Washington, D.C.: Brookings Institution, 1972).

13. Ibid., p.8.
14. Robert Smith and Harold Proshansky, *Conceptions of Work, Play, Competence and Occupation in Junior and Senior High School Students: Final Report* (Ann Arbor, Mich.: University of Michigan, Institute for Social Research, 1967), pp. 1-2.
15. Mary Engel, Gerald Marsden, and Sylvia Woodman, "Orientation to Work in Children," *American Journal of Orthopsychiatry* 38 (January 1968), pp. 137-143.
16. Eli Ginzberg et al., *Occupational Choice: An Approach to a General Theory* (New York: Columbia University Press, 1951), pp. 232-233.
17. Eli Ginzberg, "Toward a Theory of Occupational Choice: A Restatement," *Vocational Guidance Quarterly* 20 (March 1972), p. 169.
18. Ibid., p. 171.
19. Eli Ginzberg, et al., *Occupational Choice,* pp. 62-63.
20. Ibid., p. 62.
21. Herbert H. Hyman, *Political Socialization: A Study in the Psychology of Political Behavior* (Glencoe, Ill.: Free Press, 1959), chapter 2.
22. Fred I. Greenstein, *Children and Politics* (New Haven, Conn.: Yale University Press, 1965), pp. 12-15.
23. Jean Piaget and A. M. Weil, "The Development in Children of the Idea of Homeland, and of Relations with Other Countries," *International Social Science Bulletin* 3 (Autumn 1951), pp. 561-578.
24. Hyman, *Political Socialization,* chapter 2.
25. For examples of the literature of recent years on the subject of childhood socialization, see the following: R. W. Connell, *The Child's Construction of Politics* (Melbourne, Australia: Melbourne University Press, 1971); A. F. Davies, "The Child's Discovery of Nationality," *Australian and New Zealand Journal of Sociology* 4 (October 1968), pp. 107-125; Robert E. Dowse and John Hughes, "The Family, the School and the Political Socialization Process," *Sociology* 5 (January 1971), pp. 21-46; David Easton and Jack Dennis, *Children in the Political System* (New York: McGraw Hill, 1969); David Easton and Robert D. Hess, "The Child's Political World," *Midwest Journal of Political Science* 6 (August 1962), pp. 229-246; Edward S. Greenberg, "Black Children and the Political System: A Study of Socialization to Support," *Public Opinion Quarterly* 34 (Fall 1970), pp. 333-345; Fred I. Greenstein, *Children and Politics* (New Haven, Conn.: Yale University Press, 1965); Robert D. Hess and Judith V. Torney, *The Development of Political Attitudes in Children* (Garden City, N.Y.: Doubleday-Anchor Books, 1968); Dean Jaros et al., "The Malevolent Leader: Political Socialization in an American Subculture," *American Political Science Review* 42 (June 1962), pp. 564-575; Dean Jaros, *Socialization to Politics* (New York: Praeger Publishing Co., 1973); Anthony M. Orum and Roberta S. Cohen, "The Development of Political Orientations Among Black and White Children," *American Sociological Review* 38 (February 1973), pp. 62-74.
26. Robert D. Hess and Judith V. Torney, *The Development of Political Attitudes in Children* (Garden City, N.Y.: Doubleday-Anchor Books, 1968), p. 251.
27. Greenstein, *Children and Politics,* p. 1.
28. Hyman, *Political Socialization,* pp. 56-57.

29. Donald E. Super et al., *Vocational Development: A Framework for Research* (New York: Columbia University Press, 1957), p. 36.

30. For a major statement of Roe's work, see: Ann Roe, *The Psychology of Occupations* (New York: John Wiley and Sons, 1956). For a brief but more recent statement see: Anne Roe, "Perspectives on Vocational Development," in *Perspectives on Vocational Development*, ed. John M. Whitley and Arthur Resnikoff (Washington, D.C.: American Personnel and Guidance Association, 1972), pp. 61-82.

31. The discussion which follows is limited to broad generalizations about the work of Piaget. For further details, see his works, especially: *The Child's Conception of the World* (New York: Harcourt and Brace, 1959). For an excellent comprehensive view of the unifying features of Piaget's life's work, see: Mary Ann Spencer Pulaski, *Understanding Piaget: An Introduction to Children's Cognitive Development* (New York: Harper and Row, 1971).

32. Erik H. Erikson, *Childhood and Society* (New York: W. W. Norton and Co., 1963), pp. 270-274.

33. Ibid., pp. 255-256.

34. Ibid., p. 258.

35. Ibid., pp. 258-260.

36. Ibid., p. 261.

37. Robert J. Havighurst, "Youth in Exploration and Man Emergent," in *Man in a World at Work,* ed. Henry Borow (Boston: Houghton-Mifflin, 1964), p. 216.

38. Ibid., pp. 221-222.

39. In addition to the work of his colleague, Ginzberg, Super acknowledges drawing upon other works notably: C. Buehler, *Der Menschliche Lebenslauf als Psychologisches Problem* (Leipzig: Herzel, 1933) and Delbert C. Miller and William H. Form, *Industrial Sociology* (New York: Harper, 1951).

40. Super et al., *Vocational Development,* pp. 40-41.

41. Ibid., p. 40.

42. Ibid., p. 44.

43. Conditions in this inner-city school were such that after much data had been collected and coded, it became obvious to the research staff that to include these responses in the final report would be to invite unfair comparisons between these black and Puerto Rican children and those of the rest of the sample. It was readily apparent that our instruments were extremely sensitive to the verbal skills of our respondents. Substantial differences in verbal styles (both written and oral) as well as, in many instances, actual language barriers set these children apart from others in the sample. Attempts to conduct some interviews in Spanish also proved less than satisfactory, especially in several instances in which the object was to ascertain the extent to which children sex-typed occupations. With regard to this last point, the principal difficulty lay in the fact that the endings of Spanish nouns varied by gender, making the child's "choice" a moot point: e.g. *magister* is a male teacher while *magistra* is a female teacher. Finally, it must also be acknowledged that, for whatever reasons, the teaching staff at this school was consistently less cooperative than those at the other participating schools. All

things considered, fairness dictated the exclusion of these data—and the implicit comparisons which would accompany their inclusion—from this report.

44.   The decision to exclude from the analysis the responses of Johnson Heights seventh graders once again hinged on the question of fairness. Given the cooperating teacher's inability or unwillingness to control her students' behavior, the "price" for students' participation was high, namely a set of conditions under which responses could hardly have been considered willingly furnished. These children defined weekly sessions in which questionnaires were to be filled out completely (and in silence) as distasteful chores. Their responses were curt and abrupt. While their verbal abilities were comparable to those of others in the sample, their responses typically were not. The desire not to promote unfair comparisons again prompted the decision to exclude these data.

45.   For examples of other uses of this technique, see: Robert Zajonc, "Cognitive Structure and Cognitive Tuning," (unpublished Ph.D. dissertation, University of Michigan, 1955); Robert Smith and Harold Proshansky, *Conceptions of Work;* Ruth E. Hartley, "Children's Concepts of Male and Female Roles," *Merrill-Palmer Quarterly* 6 (Summer-Fall 1960), pp. 83-91.

46.   John E. Oldham, "Development of Children's Orientations to Work: A Study of Occupational Socialization," (unpublished Ph.D. dissertation, Rutgers University, 1977), pp. 92-100 and Appendix A. Or, interested parties are invited to contact the authors directly.

47.   Henry Borow, "Development of Occupational Motives and Roles," in *Review of Child Development Research,* vol. II, ed. Lois Wladis Hoffman and M. L. Hoffman (New York: Russell Sage Foundation, 1966), pp. 373-422.

48.   Joyce W. Williams, "A Gradient of Economic Concepts of Elementary Children and Factors Associated with Cognition," (unpublished Ph.D. dissertation, Florida State University, 1969).

49.   Robert Smith and Harold Proshansky, *Conceptions of Work, Play, Competence, and Occupation in Junior and Senior High School Students: Final Report* (Ann Arbor, Mich.: University of Michigan, Institute for Social Research, 1967), pp. 247-250.

50.   Claire Lipsman, "Maslow's Theory of Needs in Relation to Vocational Choice by Students from Lower Socio-Economic Levels," *Vocational Guidance Quarterly* 15 (June 1967), pp. 283-288.

51.   Fred Elkin, *The Child and Society* (New York: Random House, 1960), pp. 87-91.

52.   The most commonly employed version of Hollingshead's scale employs two factors—occupation and educational level—in assessing social position. See: August B. Hollingshead, "A Two-Factor Index of Social Position," (unpublished mimeographed paper, 1957).

Chapter 2

Children's Knowledge of the

World of Work

"In medieval society the idea of childhood did not exist . . . as soon as the child could live without the constant solicitude of his mother, his nanny, or his cradle rocker, he belonged to adult society."[1] In sharp contrast to this description provided by cultural historian Philippe Aries, ours is a very child-oriented society. Childhood is not only a socially distinct age, but one which in the more recent phases of the Industrial Age has clearly been prolonged. The movement for the establishment of child labor laws, for example, signalled the onset of an era in which children have increasingly been regarded as objects to be protected from the harsher aspects of reality.

Insofar as these "harsher" aspects may be presumed to include the social institution of work, we face an interesting sociological problem. On the one hand, educators and public officials have expressed willingness to entrust more of the responsibility for the child's work-related socialization experiences to the school. On the other hand there is little agreement on such issues as when to begin imparting such information, how much may be taken for granted, or the exist-

33

ence of benchmarks in terms of children's readiness to assimilate certain types of information. A society such as our own, which is highly work-oriented yet protective of its offspring insofar as their exposure to work is concerned, inevitably finds it necessary on occasion to monitor the effects of such countervailing tendencies upon its children. Our task in this chapter will be to survey what the children in our sample know about work and a variety of related phenomena.

Work is sufficiently pervasive as to be taken for granted by children. In the words of one seven-year-old: "Work is work. You'd better drop dead if you don't understand what work is." But as numerous studies by political scientists have shown, the fact that children take their knowledge for granted does not necessarily mean their views are accurate or even settled. Our interests here therefore include the recording and interpretation of children's misconceptions as well as the charting of their learning curves with regard to work. The focus in this chapter will be almost exclusively upon matters of cognition. The goal is to establish the existence of "baselines" of information from which children start, as well as any "plateaus" they may reach during childhood.

Our discussion of cognitive development will be restricted here to five areas of children's work orientations: (1) grasp of basic economic and commercial relationships; (2) recognition of the general role played by work in social life; (3) knowledge of selected work-related phenomena; (4) awareness of occupational role models; and (5) personal work and earning experiences. Other aspects of cognitive development will be discussed, where appropriate, in subsequent chapters of this report. The five areas of inquiry included here have been selected to illustrate a more or less general pattern of child development with regard to socialization to work. Let us examine each of these areas in turn.

Children's Grasp of Basic Economic and Commercial Relationships

Work is, among other things, an economic endeavor. Human labor is exchanged on the market; its value is determined, theoretically at least, by what the market will bear. Our first efforts to explore children's acquaintance with the world of work are therefore directed at establishing the level of children's understanding of certain basic economic and commercial relationships, most notably the principle of exchange. To ascertain the degree to which a basic economic exchange transaction was understood, we presented a hypothetical one to pupils in grades one, three, and five in the form of an inquiry from a "Man from Mars" seeking information about our way of life.[2] As early as grade one, the majority of children do grasp the depicted hypothetical situation as one of exchange. While 63 percent of first graders correctly explained the nature of the retail transaction, there was also a sizeable minority who either indicated they did not know or offered erroneous accounts of the situation. With age, however, the proportion of correct answers increased significantly. By grade five, 89 percent of pupils furnished the correct responses.

TABLE 2.1
Source of store's goods
by grade in school

	Grade in school		
Source:	1st	3rd	5th
Don't know	15.3% (28)	7.3% (14)	2.6% (5)
Named one or more elements of supply network	38.8 (71)	59.9 (115)	64.4 (125)
Store personnel make goods	12.6 (23)	10.9 (21)	2.6 (5)
All other responses	33.3 (61)	21.9 (42)	30.4 (59)
Total cases	183	192	194

$(x^2 = 49.01 \qquad p < .001)$

Neither sex, socioeconomic status, nor community of residence exerted any appreciable influence on this general pattern.

In the case of those children who failed to recognize the situation correctly, the interviewer subsequently explained that it had been a transaction in a store. All children were then asked where the store clerk might have obtained the goods for sale. Only 15 percent (28) of first graders and even fewer of those at grades three and five indicated no knowledge of such matters. Younger children were somewhat more likely to explain that store personnel make these goods themselves, but Table 2.1 suggests in general an age-related trend in favor of answers concerning a supply network of trucks and farms or factories. Again, grade in school was the sole demographic variable related to the distribution of answers.

Our next concern was with whether children recognized the principle of "agency" so often involved in retail and other transactions. If it were assumed that most store clerks do not own their respective establishments but act on behalf of the actual owners, an inquiry as to the ownership of merchandise might provide some insights into children's grasp of this economic arrangement of agency. We asked children whether the goods belonged to the clerk who was selling them. Assuming "no" to be the correct answer, the pattern of increasing awareness with age is repeated here: only 33 percent (53) of first graders said "no," compared to 62 percent (98) and 78.5 percent (139) of third and fifth graders, respectively. Again age is significantly related to the response pattern ($X^2 = 73.21$ $p < .001$). Children from the rural towns were slightly more likely to identify the seller as the owner of the merchandise. This is probably a reflection of the persistence of so-called "mom and pop stores" in these small towns.

Turning to the crux of the matter, we asked children whether it was necessary for the customer to give the salesperson the money in order to get the merchandise. The response pattern was overwhelming: Over 90 percent of children at each grade level answered in the affirmative. When the question was posed as to why this was so, our findings corroborated in general previous studies by Strauss[3] and Danziger[4] which described age-related changes in children's conceptions of the underlying rules of and rationale for exchange. Younger children did indeed tend to answer in terms of a "moral imperative," as Danziger had found. Moreover, they often also referred to the legal sanctions associated with failure to pay. For example, a seven-year-old boy said, "Yes, 'cause he has to pay for it [or] he's stealing and the alarm goes off." But other answers indicated the pattern is not universal. "Yes," said a six-year-old boy, "because food costs money and the factory needs money to make more food." With age, the likelihood of what Danziger had called a "rational economic" answer increased. That is to say, older children answered more frequently in terms of the store's need to pay suppliers and employees or to replenish inventory.

Returning to the issue of agency, certain parallels were found when children were asked whether the salesperson could not, if she chose, merely *give* products to customers. Children overwhelmingly stated that she could not, but often cited different reasons. Some responses were ritualistic. For example: "She had to follow the rules of the store—don't give anyone anything without them paying." Other answers were moralistic, such as: "Because they weren't hers!" But the greatest proportion of respondents proferred economic reasons such as: " 'Cause they have to pay the people who shipped it into the store," or "The store would probably go out of business if things were just given away." Table 2.2 shows the relative distribution of these responses by grade in school.

TABLE 2.2
Why salesperson cannot give away merchandise
by grade in school

	Grade in school		
Reason given:	1st	3rd	5th
Don't know	29.8% (50)	14.7% (29)	3.0% (6)
Economic response	29.2 (49)	44.7 (88)	35.5 (70)
Moralistic response	25.0 (42)	28.4 (56)	36.6 (72)
Ritualistic response	10.1 (17)	4.1 (8)	16.2 (32)
All other responses	6.0 (10)	8.1 (16)	8.6 (17)
Total cases	168	197	197

$$(X^2 = 68.56 \qquad p < .001)$$

These findings indicate that most children can offer a reason by first grade, and virtually all can do so by fifth grade. They also show that moralistic explanations increase slightly with age. The rise among fifth graders in ritualistic responses at the expense of economic ones may not be anomolous. It must be kept in mind that fifth graders, unlike younger pupils, completed the instrument in writing. Thus no opportunity was provided for probing. The increase in ritualistic responses may merely indicate that fifth-grade children were more likely to have taken such economic reasons for granted. Left to their own devices, they failed to see any need to elaborate beyond mere indication of the routines which have developed in view of the "obvious" underlying economic needs they satisfy.

Strauss[5] had suggested that while the five-year-old knows that the shopkeeper places money in the cash register, he is typically unclear as to both the reason for this and what happens to the cash thereafter. At about the age of seven, the child is said to distinguish between the existence of the shopkeeper's personal monetary needs and the ongoing business expenses against which receipts must be balanced. Our results do in general corroborate those of Strauss, for we found

TABLE 2.3
Percentage of pupils answering "Don't know"
by grade in school

Question:	Grade in school		
	1st	3rd	5th
Recognition of exchange transaction?	24.2%	9.4%	2.0%
Source of store's goods?	15.3	7.3	2.6
Did goods belong to salesclerk?	13.7	8.8	2.3
Why could she not give goods away?	29.8	14.7	3.0
What does she do with receipts?	7.5	2.0	2.9
How does one know price of goods?	15.9	3.0	3.0
Maximum number cases	186	302	204

increasing awareness with age of the importance of business needs, as opposed to purely personal ones, in the disposition of receipts. Children were asked to specify what the salesperson would do with the money accepted in exchange for goods. With age children increasingly indicated various business purposes rather than personal ones in their accounts of the use of receipts.[6]

Finally, we inquired of children as to how one knows how much to pay. Only one first grader in six (16 percent, $N=30$) could not offer at least a superficial explanation, i.e., that prices were marked on tags or stamped on merchandise. When probed for more ultimate explanations, however, first graders were often hard pressed to say who was responsible for pricing decisions or how they were arrived at. Many thought that the government, often in the person of the governor or president, indicated the prices stores were to charge. By third grade, however, the modal category of answers had to do with factors reasonably associated with pricing decisions: costs of labor and raw materials, demand for the product, available supply, and profit margins. A few quotes from third graders should indicate the nature of the shift. "The store manager decides by how much work and how much material it took to make it," said one child. Said another: "The man she works for decides by how much it cost him and a tiny bit more—she has to get money, too!" And finally, but hardly typically, there is this response of an eight-year-old girl with a future in economics: "The price is determined by how much of the individual product is around. If it is scarce, then the price is high. If it is plentiful, the price is lower."

Recapitulating the findings on these indicants of children's grasp of elementary economic relationships, there is evidence of a pattern which is both strong and consistent. First graders grasp more than many would no doubt give them credit for, although their "knowledge" very often includes fantasy-based misconceptions and gross oversimplifications. Third graders are a step or two closer to comprehending these economic realities. And the views of fifth graders approximate (presumed) adult views to a considerable extent. Table 2.3, which shows the proportions of students at each grade tested who answered "Don't know" to the aforementioned questions, gives a clear indication of the trend in the direction of increasing information with age.

While it is not contended that children's awareness of these selected, and rudimentary, economic issues is in itself overly significant, the pattern of increasing awareness with age is nonetheless established. Moreover neither sex, socioeconomic status, nor community of residence exerted more than low level occasional influence upon response patterns when grade in school was controlled. The pattern is clearly amenable to developmental explanation. Let us see how closely it is replicated as we turn our attention to matters more directly relevant to work.

Recognition of the General Role of Work
in Social Life

Work is among the most fundamental and pervasive categories of human activity. Consequently, it is essential that any investigation of children's work orientations attend closely to their social definitions of work. In this section, we shall focus on the "child's eye" view of work by examining its defining characteristics as children see them and children's perceptions of the significance of work in social life.

What is work? That question, when put to children in our sample,[8] elicited responses divisible into three component parts. Children see work variously as: (1) a means of getting money; (2) activity; and/or (3) a place to which one goes. Answers couched in terms of money dominated the responses, often as the sole component of the child's definition, but frequently as part of a compound answer combining two or more of the above components. Table 2.4 shows the increase, with age, in the significance of money in the child's view of work. But

TABLE 2.4
Responses to the question "What is work?"
by grade in school

Response:	Grade in school		
	1st	3rd	5th
Don't know	4.7% (9)	1.5% (3)	0.5% (1)
A means of obtaining money	35.8 (69)	55.2 (112)	57.2 (119)
Activity	11.9 (23)	11.8 (24)	9.1 (19)
A place to which one goes	6.7 (13)	3.0 (6)	1.4 (3)
Combinations of "correct" responses above	25.4 (49)	20.7 (42)	21.6 (45)
All other responses	15.5 (30)	7.9 (16)	10.1 (21)
Total cases	193	203	208

$(x^2 = 35.56$ $p < .001)$

perhaps more importantly, it also shows the ubiquity of children's recognition of the concept. Note, first of all, the paucity of "Don't know" responses even among the youngest children sampled. Moreover—if we are willing to accept that a child who furnishes one or more of the principal responses does indeed have at least a rudimentary grasp of the notion of work—we find by combining those answers that 80 percent (129) of first graders, 91 percent (184) of third graders, and 89 percent (186) of fifth graders display some understanding of the concept.

Seventh graders were asked to define work in their own words. When responses were content analyzed, the theme of "activity-for-money" emerged as the dominant response (43 percent, N=59), followed closely by "activity-without-regard-to-money" (41 percent, N=56). That "activity" was the common denominator was obvious, but the clarity of the split between pupils for whom money was or was not salient warranted further investigation. Additional analysis showed low level but consistent sex differences among children at all grade levels tested regarding the monetary aspect. Boys were consistently more likely than girls to conceive of work primarily as a means of obtaining money.

Further analysis revealed that this tendency to view work as money-producing was not significantly related to socioeconomic status, except among seventh graders. Regarding the latter, there is reason to believe that working-class children—boys especially—are by age twelve more predisposed than middle-class children to this money-oriented view of work.

In sum, a few observations are possible. First, children know from at least as early as age six or seven the meaning of work. Insofar as the salient aspects of work are concerned, it seems that work is defined by many children primarily as a means of getting money. This is somewhat more true with age, and it is more true of boys than girls. It is, however, unrelated to socioeconomic status except at seventh grade, where SES and sex presumably interact, as evidenced by the strong predisposition among working-class boys toward this response.[9]

Work, of course, is a means of attaining economic sustenance. But there are other means available as well. With this in mind, we asked children in grades one, three, and five how the "customer" in our hypothetical retail store had come by the money he was depicted as spending. As Table 2.5 suggests, the response pattern was one of early awareness of the significance of work as the source of money, but it was also one of steadily increasing awareness. That is to say, the proportion of "other" (than work) responses given by first graders was cut almost in half by grade five, whereas the proportion of children answering that the money had likely been earned by working rose from 59 percent to 81 percent. Among first graders, fantasy-ridden answers—such as that the money had come from God, or the president, or had been found, or won in the lottery—were common. By third grade, misconceptions largely took different forms, including the notions that mints and banks exist for purposes of dispensing money to people. Also apparent were instances in which children were guided by experience or observations to accept half-truths or superficial explanations. For example, one eight-year-old boy when asked how the man had gotten his money was satisfied with the literal explanation that "He probably used his Master Charge."

Working-class children were more likely to respond in terms of work as the source of money (75 percent, N=243) than were middle-class children (62 percent, N=81), but the same age-related increase applied to both groups. No differences by sex or community of residence were observed in this pattern.

TABLE 2.5
Answers to "How does one get money?"
by grade in school

Response:	Grade in school		
	1st	3rd	5th
Don't know	9.6% (18)	4.0% (8)	2.5% (5)
Earn it, work for it	58.8 (110)	71.6 (144)	80.8 (160)
All other answers	31.6 (59)	24.4 (49)	16.7 (33)
Total cases	187	201	198

$$(X^2 = 25.65 \qquad p < .001)$$

Among seventh graders, who were merely asked to explain in writing how people got money, nearly all mentioned work as a source. Many (29 percent, N=38), however, mentioned it *after* such other means of getting money as stealing and gambling, both of which figured prominently among additional responses. While there were no differences by sex among the responses of seventh graders, SES differences were once again apparent. Over three-fourths of middle-class children furnished working as their first response, compared with slightly more than half of working-class children. The latter, it would seem, are more candid about the existence of other, often extra-legal, sources of revenue. This was in contrast to the greater tendency toward work-related responses among working-class children in lower grades. Seventh graders may indeed be more world-wise than younger children, or at least more open about their cynicism.

When children were asked whether everyone worked, they exhibited nearly universal awareness of the existence of certain categories of non-workers in their communities. Over 90 percent of first graders knew that not everyone worked, and this proportion increased among older children. Most children furnished about two responses as to which categories of people were non-workers; some named as many as five. Such awareness did not vary with age, as the proportions of the various responses remained relatively constant across grade levels. Women, mothers in particular, headed the children's list of non-workers, being mentioned by 41 percent (246) of those responding. Among the younger children in the sample it was commonly held that motherhood carried an exemption from all work activities outside the home. As one six-year-old explained, "not mommies, just the daddies," worked. By third grade, however, children were qualifying this answer, noting that mothers stay home in order to care for children or do housework. Three other categories of non-workers emerged as prominent. Not surprisingly, 33 percent (196) mentioned that children do not usually work. Another 20 percent (120) mentioned the elderly or retired, of whom it was often said, to use the words of one third grader, "They're too weak." Finally, only a handful (7 percent, N=45) mentioned that the sick and crippled did not work. If this last figure seems low, it should be pointed out that, in the eyes of many respondents, being elderly meant being sick or crippled.

That children tend to define work in monetary terms and are typically able to distinguish certain categories of non-workers are hardly surprising findings. But how deeply is work impressed upon the child? How much does it count in the child's world-view? A 1939 study had found that the majority of eleven- and thirteen-year-old children sampled, when asked to picture themselves as adults, did so along occupational lines.[10] Emmerich, in a more recent study, found that five-year-olds discriminated quite effectively among "role types" in the family social structure, i.e., they differentiated between male and female parents on the basis of the relative emphasis each parental role placed upon instrumental and expressive functions.[11] Following these examples, we wondered whether being an adult was synonymous, in the eyes of children, with working. Thus, in an early interview, we asked children in grades one, three, and five what an adult (or "grown-up") was, how one came to be one, and what was involved in being one. Table 2.6 shows the predictable age-graded

TABLE 2.6
First responses to "What is an adult?"
by grade in school

	Grade in school		
Response:	1st	3rd	5th
Don't know	21.7% (38)	11.1% (21)	10.2% (21)
Involves work/job	34.9 (61)	42.6 (81)	18.0 (37)
Involves responsibilities	13.1 (23)	24.7 (47)	33.7 (69)
Involves having a family	11.4 (20)	8.9 (17)	15.6 (32)
All other responses	18.9 (33)	12.6 (24)	22.4 (46)
Total cases	175	190	205

$(X^2 = 55.95 \qquad p < .001)$

decline in "Don't know" responses. It shows, too, a more general age-trend in which younger children (grades one and three) are more apt to view adulthood somewhat narrowly, in terms of having a job, but in which, with age, a shift occurs in the direction of a broader interpretation of adulthood. The latter involves not only work, but "responsibilities" in general, i.e., the paying of bills, the giving of orders, and caring for the welfare of loved ones. Often, it includes family life—getting married and becoming a parent.

A look at some typical responses is also revealing. DeFleur had suggested that the occupational knowledge of younger children would be egocentric and concrete.[12] This proved to be true for children's conceptions of adults. A number of first graders identified adults as did this seven-year-old youth: "It's someone that takes care of you. They help if you can't reach something." Many assessed the world of the "grown-up" in the only ways they knew how, in terms of their own interests and benchmarks. "You have to be eleven or twelve," said a six-year-old girl. "You get pets!" said another. But most answered in terms of working, having responsibilities, or having a family of one's own.

Third graders evidenced such egocentrism less frequently. Instead, their responses were more abstract, more general. One girl, for example, divided grown-ups into two major categories: "You can be a mother or a father. Mothers clean house most of the time, and fathers work." Many specified what they considered to be the age of majority—ranging roughly from sixteen to thirty—or some transitional event which marks passage into adulthood: marriage, taking a job, finishing school, or moving out of one's parents' home. From this age on, the emphasis begins to broaden, taking into account various responsibilities associated with adulthood: paying bills, having to instruct and/or scold children, paying taxes, etc.[13]

Predictably, certain sex differences were found in children's social definitions of adulthood. For example, 36 percent (114) of the boys equated adulthood with working, compared to only 26 percent (65) of the girls. The latter, however, tended to be more family-oriented in their conceptions of adult social roles: 18 percent (46) of the girls defined an adult principally in terms of marital or parental status, compared to only 7 percent (23) of the boys. Since this pattern varied little across grade levels, it seems that the instrumental-expressive difference is salient to children, although perhaps not to the degree thought by many.

Further exploration of the salient dimensions of children's occupational thinking was attempted through the use of the Occupational Sorting Task, which was employed at grade levels three, five, and seven. Smith and Proshansky considered "difficulty" and "competence" as important criteria employed by children in viewing the world of work.[14] Weinstein had found that prestige was a potentially weighty factor.[15] Our intention was to test which criteria children actually employed in their occupational thinking by asking them to group thirty-three job titles[16] and thereafter recording the common denominators they reported as underlying their sorting decisions.

This procedure was directed at learning which criteria emerge spontaneously in children's thinking, not necessarily which they could have employed had they been so instructed.

The results conclusively suggest that two major dimensions dominate children's spontaneous occupational thinking. We have termed the first and most commonly employed criteria "specific activity," for it refers to the child's grouping of two or more occupations on the basis of perceived similarities in on-the-job activities. For example, children often grouped mailman, deliveryman, and truck driver, saying they all drive trucks or bring parcels. About four children in five employed this criterion in their sorting; about half used it more than once. "Occupational situs,"[17] operationalized here to include not only general economic spheres but also the *locus* of work activity, was employed nearly as frequently. The judge, the lawyer, and the police officer, for example, were often grouped together as persons involved with the law or frequently found in the courts. The teacher, the principal, and often the janitor were grouped together, as persons who would be found in schools. Many matched doctors and nurses as persons who work in hospitals, neglecting the questions of what they do or their behaviors vis-a-vis one another. Almost three children in four utilized this criterion in sorting; about half employed it more than once.

Two other occupational common denominators frequently used by children were those of "role partnership" and "similarity of tools or materials." The former refers to the complementarity of certain roles. In such cases the child went beyond merely observing that work took place in the same industry or site or noting similarities in worker behavior. He or she explained the relationship between the occupations. For example, many children explained that nurses assisted physicians during examinations or operations; other noted that bankers depend upon secretaries to take messages, etc.

Table 2.7 lists the criteria most commonly employed by children and the proportion of children who used each as a rationale for at least one of their sorting decisions. Suffice it to say that status/prestige and degree of difficulty, contrary to previously mentioned findings of others, did not emerge as particularly dominant themes. Nor did many other criteria which adults would employ in comparing occupations: requisite levels of education, the exercise of authority, sex role status, or motivation for entry into that field of work. This is not to suggest that pupils could not have sorted on these dimensions had they been asked, merely that these were less obvious or relevant to them than the aforementioned dominant responses.

TABLE 2.7
Percentage of children employing
various sorting criteria
by grade in school

	Grade in school		
Criteria Employed:	3rd	5th	7th
Specific activity (eg: drive truck, prepare food)	69.4%	88.4%	84.3%
Situs (eg: they work in health, law, etc.)	56.1	77.7	80.0
Role partnership (eg: one helps another or shares duties)	32.8	34.4	28.6
Similar tools, materials (eg: they use hand tools)	20.0	29.3	27.1
Status, prestige (eg: they are important or unimportant)	11.7	19.1	10.7
Degree of difficulty (eg: their jobs are hard or easy)	10.6	8.4	7.9
General activity (eg: they make things)	9.4	12.1	8.6
General service (eg: they help people)	8.9	7.9	12.1
Specific service (eg: they help people learn or get well)	6.1	9.3	8.6
Authority (eg: they tell others what to do)	6.7	10.2	7.1
Common employer (eg: they work for the city)	4.4	7.9	20.0
Similar motivations (eg: they do it for money, or because they like children, etc.)	2.2	4.7	1.4
Entrepreneurship (eg: they work for themselves or own it)	2.2	4.7	6.1
Sextyping (eg: these are women's jobs, men's jobs)	1.7	4.7	3.6
Similar educations (eg: they have to go to college)	1.7	3.3	7.9
Income, wealth (eg: they make a lot of money)	1.1	0.9	5.7
Total cases	180	215	140

If the four most frequently cited criteria have a common or unifying dimension, it is that they involve factors readily observable from experience. More subtle, more personal, more complex criteria are also less available for children to note. This does not explain the lack of significance of income or prestige in children's sorting behavior. Nor can we simply dismiss these as criteria of which children have no knowledge, as we shall see in chapter 5. We are forced to conclude tentatively that children in grades three, five, and seven rely less upon status or income-related criteria than upon manifest behavioral cues in viewing the world of work.

Further analysis revealed no differences of any consequence by sex, SES, or community of residence in the criteria which underlie children's occupational sorting decisions.

Our purpose in this section has been to examine children's awareness of the social significance of work. We have found that elementary school children are not vastly different from the rest of the community in this regard. They know what work is and its economic significance, at least insofar as individual sustenance is concerned. We have, however, noted certain variations with age in children's work-related cognitions. Thematic shifts in response patterns suggest that with age children's concepts of work and adult responsibilities broaden. And, there has been some indication that sex role differentiation becomes more salient in older children. We have found that even the youngest children sampled could elaborate on certain categories of non-workers. Moreover, we found that, given the opportunity to select any dimensions along which to compare occupations, children overwhelmingly settled upon similarities of activity, or situs in the broadest sense, or role partnership. These must therefore be considered more salient in the child's eye view of the world of work than, for example, income or prestige levels, or educational background, etc.

It is worth noting that there were several indicants here of children's movement from the egocentric and concretistic views to more abstract and objective views. The trend was in no sense dramatic. If anything, it may have been less pronounced than many would expect, in part because of the relatively sophisticated levels of cognition among the youngest children. But the trend was there.

Children's Knowledge of Specific
Work-Related Phenomena

Our initial efforts have been directed at describing the cognitive states of children regarding some rather broad concepts. We have examined children's developing awareness of basic economic relationships and the significance of work in our society. A fair test of cognitive development requires that our questioning also proceed along more specific lines. With this in mind, let us turn to children's knowledge of five more restrictive phenomena related to the world of work: (1) the process of getting a job; (2) their perceptions of pay differentials; (3) knowledge of occupational authority figures; (4) insight into labor disputes; and (5) understanding of welfare payments. Each will be considered in turn.

As anyone with the slightest experience in counseling college seniors can attest, it is often surprising how little prospective graduates know of the finer points of the "job hunting" process. Yet our findings suggest that even young children are aware of the *general* procedures involved in obtaining work. Perhaps we should let our younger respondents speak for themselves in testimony that this is so. The following are representative of the answers given by first and third graders to the question "How do people get jobs?"[18]:

> When someone quits, someone else replaces him. You find out about it by looking on the sign outside the place . . . The boss decides if you're good enough.
>
> Ellen, age 6

> A counselor tells them what job they have to do . . . You look for one [a job] in the city. You ask someone and they tell you if you can have it.
>
> Sharon, age 6

> You go to an office and you pick out the job you want. You ask the boss. And you tell him how old you are, and fill out papers to show how smart you are. A computer does it. The boss decides when he looks at your papers.
>
> Jeremy, age 8

> You graduate and then look for a "help wanted" sign, and ask at the place.
>
> Tommy, age 8

> You decide in college. You study it. They let you be it if you take a test.
>
> Rita, age 9

> They look in the papers. And then drive around and see the "job needed" signs. And they go in, and if they want, they take it. The manager looks to see if you do a good job, and if you do, he hires you.
>
> Keith, age 8

These responses are simplistic in that hiring decisions are rarely so automatic or clearcut as depicted, but they could hardly be called inaccurate. Most first and third graders were able to furnish some level of correct information regarding job hunting. This usually involved an explanation that one learns of the opening by seeing an advertisement in a newspaper or on a sign, then presents oneself in application. Many also elaborated on the criteria involved in the decision to hire. A small minority asserted that such decisions depended primarily on "if they like you or not." More often, pupils recognized that achieved factors play a role, citing needs for education or the passing of tests, or a trial of sorts staged so that the person hiring might decide "if you're good enough." Fifth graders seemed to take much of this for granted, with a slightly greater number (41 percent, N=76) answering instead in terms of the fit between one's interests, knowledge, skills, and/or training and the position sought. Among seventh graders,[19] the latter sort of response emerged as the dominant one (47 percent, N=49), with a re-emphasis, too, on "other" answers, including recognition of the roles of employment agencies and the like.

There is a clear age-related trend in which answers stressing getting in contact with the hiring source fade in favor of responses which stress introspection and evaluation of the goodness of fit between the job and one's interests, capacities, and qualifications. The general pattern of these results is very much in keeping with that described by Ginzberg et al.[20] in their important study of occupational choice. That is to say, there is definite developmental progress in the direction of increasing "realism," as Ginzberg would call it. But there are also some differences worthy of note. When younger children are asked how one gets a job, their answers are hardly fantasy-based, as Ginzberg presumed their occupational choices to be at ages six to eleven. Rather, they furnish reasonably accurate and objective, if incomplete, accounts of the process of job-hunting. That fifth and seventh graders apparently interpret the question somewhat differently is in itself significant, for it suggests a basic cognitive shift which likely means that many have entered the so-called "tentative period." At this stage they are prone, for the first time, to weigh potential job satisfactions versus that which the individual brings to the job. The older children in our sample were less concerned with how one finds *a* job than with how one finds *the* job he or she is suited for. Unlike the Ginzberg study—which after all asked a different question, that of occupational choice—we did not find any marked age-graded shifts in the relative emphasis fifth and seventh graders placed upon "interests" and "capacities" respectively. But we found very clear evidence of increasing realism and sophistication regarding children's knowledge of the process of linking up with a job.

TABLE 2.8
Percentages, among children giving reasons, of
explanations for pay differentials
by grade in school

	Grade in school		
Why isn't everyone's pay the same?	1st	3rd	5th
Pay varies with occupation	19.7% (24)	28.4% (50)	49.1% (85)
Some work more hours	28.7 (35)	14.8 (26)	8.1 (14)
Some work harder	51.6 (63)	56.8 (100)	42.8 (74)
Total cases	122	176	173

$$(x^2 = 43.55 \qquad p<.001)$$

As we have seen, children at all grade levels tested recognize that most people derive their incomes through work. When we broached the subject of pay with children we found nearly universal recognition of the existence of wage and salary differentials. When asked whether all workers received the same pay, 83 percent (157) of first graders, 95 percent (196) of third graders, and 96 percent (196) of fifth graders answered in the negative. Many could give no reasons for the inequities they presumed to exist but, among those who could, there could be found an obvious trend with age in the direction of realism. As Table 2.8 shows, the older children in the sample are increasingly likely to ascribe pay differentials to the nature of the job rather than to such individual factors as personal diligence or time spent on the job.

It is tempting to press the issue further, since the logical next question, namely that of *why* occupations are differentially rewarded, has long been a crucial issue within mainstream sociology.[21] We shall reserve such considerations, however, for chapter 5 of this report, which deals more generally with children's positions vis-a-vis social stratification. Here, since our concern is with cognitive development regarding the existence of pay differentials, suffice it to say that such explanations as "some work harder" and "some work longer hours" are important to children's work schemes, but give signs of crumbling by fifth grade.

It is of interest, too, to examine children's answers in relation to their socioeconomic status. Working-class children are more likely, at all grades tested, to ascribe pay differentials to individual diligence or the number of hours worked. Among working-class children who furnished reasons for the existence of pay differentials, 83 percent (215) attributed these to the above two reasons, compared to 58 percent (57) of the middle-class children who provided reasons. Whether this may be taken as an indicant of greater realism on the part of middle-class pupils is another question, however. One cannot rule out that these children are extrapolating on the basis of different types of experiences. For example, it may be that children of white collar workers hear little of the concept of "overtime," while working-class children may quite reasonably equate same with increased pay, and generalize accordingly.

That young children idealize political authority has often been interpreted as the basis of subsequent attachment to the political system.[22] But it has also been demonstrated that positive affect for political authority fades from third through ninth grade, a fact which casts doubt on the notion that early feelings are simply transferred.[23] The question has not been resolved. Here, our concern is with a parallel question, namely that of children's conceptions of occupational authority figures, i.e. "bosses." Although as it turned out cognition and evaluation are difficult to separate, our primary concern for the present lies with the former. Therefore, we began our inquiry by asking children merely "What is a boss?"

While there were a great many variations in the responses, three conceptual themes figured most prominently in the answers of children in grades one, three, and five. (The responses of seventh graders were somewhat different and will therefore be discussed separately, below.) The dominant first response, which was offered by about two or three children below grade seven, stressed the "instrumental" role of the boss. Most children conceived of the boss primarily as an instrumental leader whose role involves telling others what to do and how to do it, or controlling employees' use of time. A small minority identified the boss as an owner of the work organization. And a handful formulated their answers in terms of the status or prestige associated with the role, noting for example that, "He's the most important person," or "He gets paid the most." There were also numerous "other" responses, for the most part entirely reasonable, but a few of which recurred with any regularity among children's first answers to this question.

TABLE 2.9
Distribution of first responses to the question
"What is a boss?"
by grade in school

	Grade in school		
Response:	1st	3rd	5th
Don't know	9.5% (18)	1.0% (2)	0.5% (1)
Instrumental leader	58.5 (111)	69.0 (138)	62.4 (123)
Person with status, prestige	0.5 (1)	1.5 (3)	9.1 (18)
Owner	6.8 (13)	16.5 (33)	13.7 (27)
All other responses	24.7 (47)	12.0 (24)	14.2 (28)
Total cases	190	200	197

Table 2.9 portrays the relative distribution of these responses, as well as the "Don't know" answers among children in grades one, three, and five. While the age differences are less apparent here, it is clear that children are familiar with the concept of occupational authority: Only 9.5 percent (18) of first graders and negligible pro-

portions of older children cannot offer an explanation. But there are slight variations with age in the relative distributions of children giving each of the principal answers. After the first grade, not only do the "Don't know" responses disappear, the "Other" responses also drop off in favor of the more prominent ones. By third grade, one child in six identifies the boss as an owner; by fifth grade a few (1 percent, N=18) answer in terms of status differentials which distinguish such authority figures. With age, we see at least the beginnings of a shift from conceptualization of the boss as a social role to an economic one.[24]

This general pattern changed very little when sex, socioeconomic status, and community of residence were taken into account. Boys were in general slightly more apt to provide a status-related definition than girls (14 percent to 11 percent), but this remained a minority response at all grade levels for both sex groups.

While first responses may be assumed to be most salient in children's thinking, most furnished more than one answer here. When additional responses were taken into account, it was clear that while instrumental conceptions continue to dominate children's definitions, others emerge or disappear with age. Older children, in addition to being more likely to speak of status or ownership, also begin to mention the responsibility which falls upon the boss, as did 22.5 percent (45) of third graders, and 20 percent (40) of fifth graders. That a few first graders attend to affective aspects in defining the boss is also clear: 5 percent (9) noted that the boss is one who helps people, while 12 percent (23) defined the role as that of someone who scolded a lot or was disliked or feared. Older children did not employ such referents. The control exercised by the boss over the fate of workers also emerged in additional responses, with 12 percent (73) of children mentioning the boss' significance in hiring and firing. There were no age differences in this last matter.

Among seventh graders, who were asked essentially the same question but in a different format,[25] it was obvious that the burdensome responsibilities of the position were more salient. In fact, this category, which had not even been among the prominent first responses of younger children, rose to second place behind instrumental responses here, with 26 percent (46) of all the responses. We also asked what it is like *to be* a boss. The modal answer (35 percent, N=37) among seventh graders who responded stressed the difficulty of the role, calling it "hard work" or "a lot of trouble."

What then can be concluded from our analysis of children's conceptualizations of occupational authority? In order to answer this, our findings must be considered in relation to those of previous studies. Danziger had explored the concept of the boss in children five to eight years of age;[26] Haire and Morrison had done the same with respondents in grades seven through eleven.[27] The former had found even the youngest children sampled quite conversant with the term, as we have. We are also able to corroborate the general pattern discerned by Danziger of a shift from answers in terms of purely social functions of the boss to those describing economic functions. In our sample, however, this transition was far from complete, as even among seventh graders instrumental role activities dominated children's social definitions. The economic role of the boss as owner and source of wages and the status and higher salary associated with the role were, to be sure, more prominent among the older children, but not dominant themes. Nor did we find the pronounced differences by SES which had characterized the Haire and Morrison study of children in grades seven and up. We did, however, note slight, but not statistically significant, differences in this regard, with middle-class children somewhat more given to the instrumental, responsibility, and status themes, while working-class children were slightly more inclined to view the boss as the source of wages and the one who hires and fires. It would seem that the SES differences found by Haire and Morrison come to prominence during the high school years.

The final two work-related phenomena to be considered in this section present us with a departure from the pattern of gradual but steady cognitive development we have seen thus far. For it is only when we examine children's knowledge of labor disputes and welfare that we find, for the first time, a suggestion of the existence of "threshold effects" in children's work orientations. That is to say, here we encounter evidence which suggests a clear age-related demarcation: a certain age prior to which very few children grasp the concept, but beyond which it is understood by most.

It is crystal clear that for the majority of children sampled recognition of the nature of labor disputes comes between third and fifth grade. As Table 2.10 shows, there is a forty percentage-point leap in the correct response rates at that point. This suggests either a dramatic increase in "readiness" to grasp this notion of labor disputes by grade five or some unexplained increase in older children's experiential exposure to the term and consequent understanding of it.

During the elementary years, children progress from virtually no knowledge of strikes in first grade to the opposite extreme, at which nearly all seventh graders can render a reasonable account of the concept. The youngest children were unable to account for the depicted hypothetical situation of men with signs picketing a factory to keep others from entering. About three in five drew blanks. The bulk of the remainder resorted to a variety of explanations, especially that of a disaster of some sort—a fire, an explosion, theft, a leak, a fuel shortage, or even the death of a child within the building—which prevented the plant from operating. Some grasped that such actions as were depicted are often taken in protest, citing noise levels or

TABLE 2.10
Children's recognition of strikes
by grade in school

| | Grade in school | | | |
Response:	1st	3rd	5th	7th
Don't know	59.2%	42.6%	6.0%	---
	(100)	(80)	(13)	(0)
Misconceptions	31.9	18.6	15.2	4.5
	(54)	(35)	(33)	(6)
Identified labor dispute	8.9	38.8	78.8	95.5
	(15)	(73)	(171)	(127)
Total cases	169	188	217	133

$$(x^2 = 32.11 \qquad p < .001)$$

pollution or attributes of the personal behavior of the boss as the reasons for same. Fewer than one in ten first graders, however, answered that the men were striking, i.e., that they were refusing to work due to a disagreement with management over wages or conditions. When asked if they had heard the term "strike" over 90 percent indicated they had not, at least not in its present context.

By third grade the term had passed into the recognition vocabularies of a distinct minority of children. The frequency of misconceptions decreased and some children could indeed answer on an informed basis. Nine-year-old Jonathan, while somewhat atypical, is a case in point. He understood picketing as an effort to make management an offer it could not refuse:

It's a strike. [Why?] They wanted something—more money, a raise, a better place—and the boss wouldn't give it to them. And they wanted it. And they didn't want anyone to get into their place. So the boss could go out of business, or give it to them.

Such an answer was relatively rare among third graders. It was, however, typical among the responses of fifth graders, 70 percent (155) of whom supplied the terms "strike" or "picketing" in their accounts of the depicted situations. Haire and Morrison, who had also explored knowledge of strikes in grades seven through eleven, had noted that seventh and eighth graders tended to personalize labor disputes, "to see issues and rights and wrongs as residing in the persons of the protagonists."[28] In light of the present findings, such an appraisal seems relativistic indeed. We have no doubt that, in comparison with the responses of high school students, the views of seventh and eighth graders did in fact seem simplistic due to personalization. But if one examines conceptualizations of labor disputes on an age continuum starting with first graders, the responses of fifth and seventh graders stand out as relatively abstract. Younger children who had understood that a labor dispute was at issue often attributed it to the anger or recalcitrance of one or both parties. Among older children in our sample, such accounts often centered on the leverage which a work stoppage was intended to exert upon management, etc. There was most definitely an observable age-related trend during the elementary years in the direction of increasingly abstract and sophisticated understanding of labor disputes. Moreover, that age was the most significant variable was attested to by our findings of no significant relationship between conceptions of strikes and the variables of sex, SES, and community of residence.

When children were asked to evaluate whether most strikes are right or wrong, two further observations were possible. First, with age children tend to gather enough information to formulate opinions on the matter. Only ten first graders both perceived the situation as a strike and expressed opinions regarding its propriety. The proportion of children at each grade level satisfying both conditions rose steadily thereafter, with the third-to-fifth-grade difference, predictably, shifting the plurality to those with opinions. Second, among children who had such opinions there was a tendency, as Table 2.11 shows, to consider strikes right. This did not shift significantly with age. It is of interest to note also that a substantial minority of children in grades, three, five, and seven indicated conditional answers, saying "it depends," or "they're right if . . ." or "they're wrong if . . ." in most of these cases, the conditions specified were monetary, i.e., depending upon whether or not wage levels were fair, or the employer's ability to pay.

TABLE 2.11
Distribution of expressed opinions regarding whether strikes are right or wrong by grade in school

Opinion expressed:	Grade in school[31]		
	3rd	5th	7th
Strikes are right	41.3% (31)	48.4% (74)	50.4% (61)
Strikes are wrong	34.7 (26)	23.5 (36)	22.3 (27)
Conditional answers	24.0 (18)	28.1 (43)	27.3 (33)
Total cases	75	153	121

$$(x^2 = 4.35 \qquad p = ns)$$

Haire and Morrison had earlier noted pronounced SES difference in students' evaluations of strikes. They had found that by seventh grade response patterns were already well established: Middle-class youngsters overwhelmingly thought strikes wrong, while working-class youth felt them to be, if not right, at least necessary.[29] Here, we found much more modest differences. At grades three and five, higher SES children were more likely than others to have formulated their opinions in conditional terms rather than to have expressed unequivocal opposition to strikes.[30] In fact, strikes were viewed as at least potentially acceptable by the majority of children of both SES groups at all grade levels tested. Surprisingly, no significant differences by SES were found in the response patterns of seventh graders. Whether the dissimilarities between our findings and those of Haire and Morrison can be accounted for by differences in the composition of the samples or the sixteen-year time lag or some other factors cannot be estimated here. It is, however, certain that the opinions of these children were far less organized along predictable ideological lines, by SES, than were those of the somewhat older group examined by Haire and Morrison.

While no significant sex difference had emerged in the opinions of third and fifth graders regarding the propriety of strikes, this was a factor in the responses of seventh graders. Boys were significantly more disposed toward viewing strikes as right whereas girls were more tentative, expressing their opinions more frequently in conditional terms.[32]

TABLE 2.12
Responses to question "What is welfare?"
by grade in school

Response:	Grade in school			
	1st	3rd	5th	7th
Don't know	91.9%	73.8%	20.6%	4.9%
	(159)	(144)	(41)	(5)
"Correct" responses	5.8	15.9	51.8	65.6
	(10)	(31)	(103)	(67)
Misconceptions	2.3	10.3	27.6	29.4
	(4)	(20)	(55)	(30)
Total cases	173	195	199	102

$(x^2 = 473.20 \qquad p < .001)$

Our final effort to explore children's knowledge of work-related phenomena involved the issue of welfare payments. Again, we found very few first graders conversant with the concept. "My father tells me everything," said seven-year-old Gene, "but I've never heard of that one!" Over 90 percent of first graders shared his lack of knowledge. By third grade the distribution had changed little, although there were a smattering of "correct" responses.[33] As Table 2.12 shows, however, the previous findings of a quantum leap in awareness of strikes from third to fifth grade was replicated here with regard to knowledge of welfare. But such knowledge was in general neither as extensive nor as widespread as had been awareness of labor disputes. Among fifth graders, for example, about half could furnish a correct response; among seventh graders, about two-thirds could do so.[34]

It is of interest to note that while the proportion of "Don't know" responses decreased with age, largely in favor of correct information, the proportion of misconceptions also rose steadily. Our interpretation is that this pattern attests to the existence of incremental increases in awareness or, if you will, progressive stages of understanding quite possibly indicative of growing readiness to grasp the concept. A few examples will clarify this. First graders either admit to no recognition of the term, or merely surmise from the context of the question that it has to do with money. Only a very few could specify for whom the money was intended or the rationale for the practice. Among some third graders, welfare was often equated with charity or even with the practice of extending credit. Nine-year-old William identified welfare as: "When people come over and help you when you're poor. They do things for you, like get rid of the rats. [Who does?] The rich people." Eight-year-old Jerry said, "When you're poor, you get money. And after you get a job, you pay them back. [Where does the money come from?] The taxes people pay." Thus, some third graders grasped at least the gist of the matter, even if their conceptions may have been muddled or simplistic.

Many fifth graders evidenced a more complex understanding of the matter. Not only had the "Don't know" responses dropped off greatly, but pupils were typically able to name categories of persons believed eligible as welfare recipients. It was also obvious that many confused welfare with other programs of social insurance, especially unemployment insurance, social security payments to the retired or disabled, death benefits paid to surviving families either by the government or by private firms, even union strike benefits. The common denominator, that welfare represents financial help for those facing hard times, was relatively well understood, although the details may have been confused. Seventh graders were the most likely to supply such information. In fact, most of them (65 percent, N=66) furnished multiple responses regarding imputed categories of eligible welfare recipients, including: the poor, the disabled, children in fatherless homes, large families with inadequate means of support, the elderly, the sick, those temporarily out of work, and, finally, those too lazy to work. While many of these answers are technically incorrect, they nonetheless suggest the growth of social awareness of the world of work.

We found no differences in children's knowledge of welfare by sex or community of residence. One would, however, expect differences in such awareness by SES, if only because middle-class families may be presumed to have less first-hand contact with welfare and are presumably less outspoken on the issue within the home. This was found not to be the case, however, until grade seven, at which time low SES children display somewhat greater awareness of the concept than did middle-class children.[35]

It should be noted, however, that the SES split in this sample is between middle-class and working-class children, often from the same communities. There are few children from "poverty areas" represented, and to our knowledge only a handful of children from families receiving welfare. That first-hand experience with welfare is an important contributor to knowledge of the concept is eloquently attested to by the following interview with Kevin, a nine-year-old from one of the rural communities:

I: Do you know what welfare is, Kevin?

R: My dad's on welfare. And when we go to school, you get tickets and get free lunches. And sometimes, when you don't have a mother, the welfare . . . [He pauses, losing train of thought.]

I: [Changing the subject] Does everyone get welfare?

R: No, because some people don't like welfare.
     [He then stresses that his father appreciates it, and that he does not know why others look down upon it.]

I: Do you know why some people get it?

R: No, but my dad gets it and other people do, too.

I: Where does it come from?

R: It's from "The Welfare." Your dad pays half and the Welfare pays half—for the babysitter. So when you need a babysitter [He means day care service.] You don't have to spend all that money. The Welfare pays half.

This last point, illustrative of children's vague allusions to the source of welfare payments, points up another aspect of their general pattern of awareness of the phenomena. Only one first grader could correctly identify the government as the source of such payments. Among third graders who had attempted an explanation, only 29 percent (15) had "correctly" identified the source, citing either the government, the state, the city, or tax revenues in their answers. By fifth grade, this figure had risen to 51 percent (81) of those attempting an explanation; by seventh grade it was 90 percent (87). The range of misconceptions in this regard was greatest among fifth graders, one of whom, for example, explained that those who could afford to do so purchased policies from Mutual of Omaha, which subsequently made welfare payments if they were needed.

As had been the case with children's opinions regarding strikes, older children proved not only better informed concerning the nature of welfare, but more inclined to evaluate it as well. Children were asked their opinions on whether they were "for" or "against" welfare. Admittedly, since we have already established that children perceived welfare as a benefit to the unfortunate, this was a loaded question. The "pro" responses far outweighed the "cons." But the former diminished somewhat with age in favor, not of negative answers, but conditional responses.

In order to ascertain children's opinions regarding welfare, we posited a hypothetical situation in which two men argued its "pros" and "cons." We then asked children which person they thought was right. Among young children, support of the welfare program tends to be unequivocal, largely because the perceived stakes were so high. "If they don't get enough money," said eight-year-old Jimmy of welfare recipients, "they could die." For ten-year-old Sandra, who claimed several of her neighbors are on welfare, the threat is very real. "The one for welfare [was right]," she said, "because they need to take care of them, so they don't die." For Stanley, age six, the logic of the practice was evident: "Some people don't got enough money to buy things, like food . . . some people would die if they didn't have welfare, 'cause they wouldn't have enough money to buy food." For others, like eleven-year-old Bryan, there is a moral imperative involved: "[the one] for it [was right], because he wants to help people who aren't as well off as themselves." Still others think of the social consequences of doing away with the program. "If there weren't welfare," observed a fifth grade girl, "people would be outside roaming the streets."

The older children, however, tended to qualify their evaluations. "If everyone got it, the world would be a big mess," noted ten-year-old Andrea, who nonetheless supported the concept, ". . . because if there was no welfare, we would have beggars, and people living in the middle of the street." Most supported the practice, but "only for the people that need it—that don't have a job and they're poor," to borrow the words of ten-year-old Diane. "If you're not very sick or very hurt," offered a male classmate, then as far as he was concerned, "you don't get it!"

Very few shared the opinion of ten-year-old Eddie, who described welfare as "getting money free," and said he opposed it on grounds that, "People have to work for their money." Such pejorative views of welfare recipients, presumably common among adults, were not found to any significant degree among the children sampled.

In conclusion of this section, lest anyone remain tempted to dismiss all elementary children as ill-informed or incapable of understanding the matters discussed in these pages, we offer the thoughts of a remarkably well informed fifth grade girl:

> I: Do you know what welfare is, Laura?
> R: Welfare is money given out to people that don't have jobs and can't get jobs.
> I: Where does it come from?
> R: The government.
> I: Which person do you think was right, the one for welfare or the one against it?
> R: I think the one for it, because without welfare how would these people be able to live? They wouldn't be able to buy food. The only other thing they could get would be unemployment, and they would need a job for a little while for that.

Enough said. Let us go on to consider other aspects of children's work orientations.

Children's Awareness of Occupational Role Models

Socialization, especially during childhood, must be thought of as a process of psychosocial development geared toward conferring upon the individual the various identities needed to equip his social self for the road ahead. Among these is an "occupational identity," said to have been acquired when one evidences "a concept of himself as a worker with a career," as Havighurst once put it.[36] But this is frosting, a phenomenon of late adolescence built upon the foundation of successful completion of prior "occupational developmental tasks." The first of these, "identification with a worker," has been considered largely confined to the elementary school years.[37] It will be our task in this section to explore a restricted but important aspect of the critical process of identification, namely the child's awareness of occupational role models.

The most obvious, and most significant, role models of early and middle childhood are parents. It is not our purpose here to comment on the nature of parental influence upon children's occupational development, for that has been amply explored elsewhere.[38] Rather, we shall continue our investigation of key aspects in the child's cognitive development, seeking patterns of children's awareness of parental occupational roles.

TABLE 2.13

**Knowledge of father's work
by grade in school***

	Grade in school			
Level of knowledge:	1st	3rd	5th	7th
	(interviews)		(written)	
Low knowledge (0-4 points)	35.5% (72)	19.9% (40)	19.5% (42)	6.4% (8)
Moderate knowledge (5-8 points)	56.7 (115)	52.7 (106)	60.0 (129)	53.6 (67)
High knowledge (9-12 points)	7.9 (16)	27.4 (55)	20.5 (44)	40.0 (50)
Total cases	203	201	215	125

$(x^2 = 44.59 \qquad p<.001)$

* First and third graders were interviewed. Fifth and seventh graders answered in writing, providing no opportunity for interviewer probing.

In order to test children's awareness of parental occupational activity, a "depth of information" scale was devised. Children's scores, ranging from zero to twelve points, were calculated on the basis of depth of information provided with respect to whether parents worked, the locus and nature of the work, and the job title.[39] Separate scores were calculated for children's knowledge of paternal and maternal role models. Table 2.13 shows a slight but significant pattern of increasing awareness with age of knowledge of the father's work.

As the table suggests, what we have called "moderate" awareness was the mode at all grades tested. The differences were found in the age distributions of scores at either end of the scale: with age, a higher level of awareness became in general more likely, while the proportions of low scores diminished. This pattern was relatively unaffected by sex, community of residence, or socioeconomic status— each of which was found not to be significantly related to awareness of father's occupation. These last facts may prove interesting in light of the attention traditionally paid to children's identification with like-sex parents,[40] and the imputed tendencies by working-class families to downplay aspects of paternal work roles lest strong identification inhibit children's aspirations for upward mobility.[41] Among elementary school children at least, we found no indication that such factors make any difference in rudimentary knowledge of paternal occupational activity.

Assigning some meaning to these quantified age-related differences we have observed requires an examination of the responses upon which these scores are based. The following are reconstructed from actual excerpts in which two respondents, a first and a seventh grader, respectively, discussed the nature of their father's work. Our first respondent was interviewed, the second replied in writing to the same questions, minus the probes.

Case one: George, 6 years old, grade one

I: George, does your father work?
R: Yes.
I: Would it be okay with you if I asked you some questions to see how much you can tell us about your dad's work?
R: Yes.
I: What is your father's job?
R: He works at *Today's Medicine.*
I: Do you know where that is?
R: It's in Exeter, and in New York. And all places.
I: And do you know what they call someone who does what he does?
R: No.
I: Do you know what he does when he's working?
R: He sits down at a desk and has pages to read.
I: Do you kow anything else about your dad's work?
R: Not really.

Case two: Stanley, 12 years old, grade seven

Q: My father's job is——.
A: Sales manager (eastern)
Q: The name of the place where my father works is——.

A: Continental Plastics Co.
   Park Avenue, N.Y., N.Y.
Q: Things my father does when he is working are——.
A: He calls stock brokers, takes care of his salesmen, writes reports, and goes on lots of business trips to other cities for meetings and demonstrations.

The above could hardly have been called "typical" of either first or seventh graders, for the first would have scored slightly below the modal category, while the second would have been above the norm. They do, however, serve our purposes here, since they illustrate on a qualitative basis the differences in children's awareness. For exam-

TABLE 2.14
Knowledge of mother's work
by grade in school*

	Grade in school			
Level of knowledge:	1st	3rd	5th	7th
	(interviews)		(written)	
Low knowledge (0-4 points)	23.0% (17)	16.1% (15)	21.4% (22)	6.8% (4)
Moderate knowledge (5-8 points)	66.2 (49)	48.4 (45)	58.3 (60)	55.9 (33)
High knowledge (9-12 points)	10.8 (8)	35.4 (33)	20.4 (21)	37.3 (22)
Total cases	74	93	103	59

$$(X^2 = 22.58 \qquad p<.01)$$

* First and third graders were interviewed. Fifth and seventh graders answered in writing, providing no opportunity for interviewer probing.

ple, the father of six-year-old George may be a magazine director, or he may be a copy boy. One could not be sure purely on the basis of the information George could supply. Stanley's account, on the other hand, leaves little to chance. His description of his father's work activities differs markedly from George's in terms of its specificity. And it is that dimension which separates the younger from the older children here. First and third graders tend to know where their fathers work and the general nature of their contributions. Fifth and seventh graders can be far more specific. For example, one rural twelve-year-old, whose father was a foundry worker, explained in some detail the process of blending copper with other molten metals to form the alloy bronze. Another explained the duties of department store controller, including writing job descriptions and instruction manuals for employees, planning the locations and building plans for new stores, and improving existing "systems." Finally, there is the case of the twelve-year-old son of a food vending machine supplier, who even listed all the towns on his father's route.

TABLE 2.15
Mean scores on depth of information
of parental occupations
by grade in school

	Grade in school			
Level of knowledge:	1st	3rd	5th	7th
	(interviewed)		(written)	
Knowledge of father's work (mean in points)	3.58	6.66	6.36	7.70
Total cases	203	201	215	125
Knowledge of mother's work (mean in points)	6.09	7.17	6.33	7.98
Total cases	74	93	103	59

Turning to the issue of children's awareness of their mother's work, a few observations are in order. In the first place, it is clear that many children do not conceive of being a housewife or mother as "work." About two in five of them answered that their mothers did not work, but kept house and raised children. Less than half as many children (44 percent, N=329) reported employed mothers as had earlier reported employed fathers. Table 2.14 reports on awareness of employed mothers' work, showing that the general pattern found earlier with respect to knowledge of father's work also prevailed here. That is to say, moderate knowledge of the work activities of employed mothers was the mode at all grade levels, with low knowledge yielding in general in favor of high knowledge by grade seven. Again, neither sex, nor community of residence, nor socioeconomic status was significantly related to such awareness.

While we cannot say whether the mother's or father's work activities are more important in terms of the child's work-related cognitive development, it is possible to compare children's awareness of the two, in the hope of finding some clues. Table 2.15 arrays the mean depth of information scores, by grade, for awareness of father's and mother's occupations. It is clear that first graders evidence higher awareness of maternal work roles than they do paternal ones. This may be attributable to younger children's having greater exposure to their mothers,[42] or to some other factor. In any event, this effect disappears. By grade three and beyond the means are nearly comparable. Nor do sex, community of residence, or SES influence this pattern. Evidently, beyond grade one, children are about equally aware of the occupational activities of working parents of either sex.

TABLE 2.16
Knowledge of maternal work roles by
mother's occupational status

Level of knowledge:	Job status of working mother	
	Managerial/ professional	Working class
Low knowledge (0-4 points)	2.0% (1)	0.9% (1)
Moderate knowledge (5-8 points)	63.2 (31)	74.4 (87)
High knowledge (9-12 points)	34.7 (17)	24.8 (29)
Total cases	49	117

$$(x^2 = 2.25 \qquad p = ns)$$

One qualification should be placed upon the above conclusion. While it is true that socioeconomic status was not significantly related to awareness of the occupational activities of either parent, it should be kept in mind that SES has been operationalized in this study as a function of father's occupation and community of residence. One might therefore legitimately wonder whether the occupational levels of working mothers do not influence their children's awareness of maternal work roles. Indeed we found, as Table 2.16 shows, that children of mothers working at higher occupational levels were slightly but not significantly better informed about their mothers' work roles than were their peers whose mothers had working class jobs.[43] We have little evidence, therefore, that professional women's roles are better known to their children than are the work activities of working class employed mothers.

We conclude this brief analysis of children's knowledge of the occupational roles of their parents with two observations. In the first place, children are relatively well informed about the generalities of parental occupational behavior, and their levels of awareness increase slightly with age. Further, the pattern is primarily age-related, and shows little evidence whatsoever of being influenced by even such variables as sex or SES, which would have been thought to influence such cognitions.

Children's Work and Earning Experiences

As we consider particular findings relating to children's work orientations, we should keep in mind the initial reasons which prompted this investigation, namely the desire to explore the childhood socialization process as it applies to work. No discussion of cognitive growth would be complete without consideration of the experiential factors related to cognition. Children's knowledge of work can hardly be separated from their work experiences. In this section, therefore, we present information on children's early ventures into the world of work. Rather than attempt to discern causal links or associations between experiential and cognitive aspects of children's work orientations, we shall concentrate instead on establishing the existence of certain parallels between the two. Our principal task in this chapter, it should be recalled, involves the search for cognitive patterns. How do children's work experiences fit into the mosaic we have thus far been trying to construct? That is the issue at hand.

The investigation of that question will proceed by examining three aspects of children's work-related experiences: allowance, chores, and extra-familial work. Each will be considered in turn.

The parental practice of giving "allowances" to children is a most interesting phenomenon indeed. From the standpoint of the analysis of children's work orientations, it may be of great significance. Most parents do, after all, provide *in toto* for the financial support of at least their younger children. Whether the child handles any of the money or merely has his wants administered to by an indulgent parent would largely be a matter of indifference were it not for their conviction that something more is at stake. Nor can the fact that allowances are often given in exchange for the child's performance of certain domestic activities be accepted as the ultimate explanation for the practice. To consider the child's compliance with such requests as totally contingent upon receipt of a monetary reward ignores the nature of the familial household, which (1) cannot be compared to the abstract labor market, since the child rarely has an alternative in terms of where to sell his labor; and (2) depends much more upon non-monetary rewards—such as love, filial responsibility, etc.—than upon cash in the matter of motivating children to be helpful. Rather, we are inclined to think, parents view the practice within the context of the general "money education" of their children, as Marshall and Magruder have called it.[44] In their 1960 survey of the parents of rural Kentucky students in grades seven through twelve, these authors concluded that many parental money education practices were positively related to children's knowledge and use of money. They even went so far as to develop a list of recommended parental practices which stated, among other things, that giving children more money to spend and to save enhanced their growth in terms of both awareness of money and its proper use.

Our interest here revolves around such matters as the proportion of children at each age level who receive allowances, and the implications of the ways in which allowances are paid. Regarding the former, we found that nearly half the children in the sample regularly receive an allowance starting at least as early as grade one. By grade three, this proportion increased to about three in five, where it apparently levels off. This plateau effect may be attributable, as we shall see later, to the fact that some fifth and seventh graders either (1) are dropped from the allowance rolls upon being considered capable of earning money outside the home, or (2) re-define money received at home as "wages" for increased chore activities expected in some households. The age-graded pattern depicted is not subject to variation by sex, and it seemed to vary little by either SES or community of residence.[45]

When we turn our attention to the matter of *how much* children receive for their allowance, we learn, first of all, that this figure is a constant one. While about one child in sixteen reported above that he or she does not always get an allowance, only 2 percent (8) of those reporting the amount received said it varied. In other words, while there may be some weeks in which the sum is not forthcoming, parents are apparently quite consistent about the amount of the allocation. Moreover, we found no significant differences by SES in the size of children's allowances. That the family's ability to pay is apparently not a factor in the size of this figure, and that the constancy of the sum should be such a prominent finding may imply that there is more involved in the practice than merely seeing that the child's wants are satisfied. We surveyed children, not parents, so we can do no more than speculate, but it would appear that the sum of the child's allowance, once established, is "sacred"—to the parents because of the value they may impute to the child's learning to responsibly budget fixed sums, and certainly to the children, who typically demonstrate a strong affinity for consistency.

TABLE 2.17
Reported allowance figures per week
by grade in school

| Reported weekly allowance: | Grade in school* | | | |
	1st	3rd	5th	7th
$0.25 or less	43.9% (43)	18.6% (24)	6.3% (9)	---
$0.26 to $0.99	14.3 (14)	38.0 (49)	29.4 (42)	14.9 (13)
$1.00 to $1.99	27.6 (27)	36.4 (47)	44.8 (64)	42.5 (37)
$2.00 or more	14.3 (14)	7.0 (9)	19.6 (28)	42.5 (37)
Total cases reporting amounts	98	129	143	87

$$(X^2 = 111.03 \qquad p<.001)$$

* Percentages based upon number of children at each grade level reporting the amount of allowances received.

The size of the allowance does, however, tend to vary with age, as Table 2.17 clearly shows. While not all children report receiving their allowance on a weekly basis—some receive it daily, biweekly, or even monthly—this chart converts all such reports to weekly sums, arrayed by grade in school. Note, first, the clearly visible "graduated" effect of the distribution. Note also—and this may prove disconcerting for those of us whose cohorts matured in times less pinched by inflation—that the modal category across all cases of children reporting the size of their allowance is between one and two dollars per week.

TABLE 2.18

**Percentage of children reporting regular performance
of selected commonly reported chores
by grade in school***

		Grade in school		
Chores:	1st	3rd	5th	7th
Help with housework	49.3% (101)	48.5% (99)	51.6% (112)	53.0% (70)
Clean own room, make bed	42.4 (87)	52.9 (108)	54.8 (119)	52.3 (69)
Wash/dry dishes	18.0 (37)	24.5 (50)	30.9 (67)	30.3 (40)
Remove trash	13.2 (27)	30.4 (62)	34.6 (75)	37.9 (50)
Yardwork	14.1 (29)	8.8 (18)	12.0 (26)	29.5 (39)
Pet care	9.3 (19)	18.1 (37)	27.6 (60)	22.0 (29)
Other: errands, babysit, set table, help with cooking, etc.	27.3 (56)	30.4 (62)	25.8 (56)	18.9 (27)
Total cases	205	204	217	132

* Percentages may add to more than 100% because most
  children report regular performance of at least two chores.

Allowance, we found, was very rarely unconditionally granted by parents. Most children reported the performance of routine household chores on a regular basis, presumably as their means of "earning" their allowances. But chores were often a part of life for even those children not receiving allowance. For example, 79.5 percent (163) of all first graders sampled reported having chores to do, and that figure rose slightly with age. This general pattern did not significantly differ by sex or community of residence, nor were the SES differences, while statistically significant, particularly substantial.[46] There was also a clear age progression regarding the number of chores typically reported by children. But its range was narrow, with first graders averaging two chores and seventh graders about three. Table 2.18, which shows the distribution by grade in school of children's reported performance of the most common household chores, suggests that chores are allocated on an additive, rather than purely age-graded basis. That is to say, the fact that most of the rows in the table show substantial age-related increases, may indicate that children do not "outgrow" certain chores, but merely accumulate additional ones with age.

Ours is an age, many would have us believe, in which the importance of ascriptive status, especially sex, in the allocation of work activities is on the decline. Without data on the allocation of chores among cohorts of previous eras, and without controlling for the number and sex of other siblings in the households of the children sampled, it would of course be impossible to make any definitive statements as to the exact implications of our findings relative to the distribution by sex of reported chores among these children (see Table 2.19). However, by whatever standards one wished to apply to the interpretation of these data (which were collected in 1973-74), it would be difficult indeed to maintain that they describe an allocation system in which sex roles were unimportant. The findings below make it quite clear that during childhood, even in the 1970s, sex roles play an important part in the allocation of and/or self-selection into performance of household chores. How else, for example, could the ratio of girls to boys reporting doing dishes be in excess of three to one? Or the similar ratio for helping with housework be nearly two or one? How else could it be that the percentage of boys reporting taking out the trash could be nearly four times the girls' percentage?[47]

Sociologically, we need not be surprised at such findings. Sex, along with age, has been a dominant factor in the allocation of adult work roles in nearly all human societies throughout the ages. That such a time-honored, indeed seemingly "natural" process should persist in our culture into an era just now beginning to pay lip service to sexual egalitarianism, and only in some quarters, should hardly be cause for a raised sociological eyebrow. We mention it here, in the midst of consideration of children's cognitive development regarding work orientations, merely as a sobering thought to those among us who would point to present child rearing practices as proof positive that a new order has come.

Havighurst had stressed the significance of "acquiring the basic habits of industry" as one of the preeminent developmental tasks facing children ages ten to fifteen.[48] Learning to accept chores, allocate one's time, and perform them acceptably was considered an

TABLE 2.19
Percentage of children reporting regular performance of selected commonly reported chores by sex*

Chores:	Sex	
	Boys	Girls
Help with housework	35.2% (143)	67.9% (239)
Clean own room/make bed	43.8 (178)	58.2 (205)
Wash/dry dishes	13.8 (56)	39.2 (138)
Remove trash	41.9 (170)	11.6 (41)
Yardwork	23.6 (96)	5.1 (18)
Pet care	22.9 (93)	14.8 (52)
Other: errands, babysit, set table, help with cooking, etc.	19.7 (80)	32.7 (115)
Total cases	406	352

* Percentages may add to more than 100% because most children reported regular performance of at least two chores.

essential aspect of work-related growth during the elementary school years. So was developing the ability to discriminate when it was appropriate to put work before play.[49] Most children, even prior to the age at which Havighurst would suggest we attend to such behavior, report regular performance of more than one household chore.

Further, most also report the occasional performance of "special jobs" for parents or other members of the family.[50] These, it turns out, refer to matters demanding only infrequent attention, like raking leaves in autumn or turning up the garden soil in springtime. "Chores," on the other hand, are typically viewed as regular, repetitive tasks performed almost daily. In addition, it seems "special jobs" are tasks one is *asked* to do, whereas "chores" are socially defined within the culture of childhood as things one is *expected* to do. Thus, what is a special job for one child may be a chore for another. The existence of this residual category of tasks explains, for example, the relatively low proportion of children who named yardwork among their chores. For about half the boys (and for one girl in four) yardwork came under the heading of a special job. Many younger children did not report helping with housework when asked for a list of their chores, but did not hesitate to include it as an "extra" task or a "sometimes job," as many called it. That babysitting had not figured more prominently among the chores of fifth and seventh grade girls seemed puzzling, until nearly half of them were found to define it in this way. The same was true of running errands, placed in this category by a distinct minority of children of both sexes.

It is important to distinguish between the work which the child does as part of his or her family responsibilities and the phenomenon of "childwork." This term was employed by Engel and her colleagues in reference to work performed by children at one time or another for strangers for pay.[51] The significance of such experience has been emphatically underscored by Borow, who ranked "outside work experiences" first among four precipitants of occupational choice which emerged in retrospective discussions with subjects asked who or what had been the chief influences upon their career decisions.[52] This is not by any means to suggest that *what* children do will necessarily prove a good predictor of later occupational behavior. As Engel et al. recognized, the number of job opportunities open to children is very narrow indeed, and is very often determined by social factors. Nor does it resemble even remotely the occupational spectrum of the adult world. What *is* important, they have asserted, is that the child's experiences be such that he has the opportunity to develop a multi-faceted "work-style" which will presumably stand him in good stead with regard to his later relationships with the world of work.[53]

Here, we adopted a slightly more liberal definition of childwork than had originally been employed by Engel et al. We used the concept in reference to all of the child's paid work experiences outside the household of the family of origin. We endeavored in our coding decisions to restrict the use of the term to "regular," although not necessarily continuous, tasks. Thus, any child who indicated that he or she had ever entered into an employer-employee relationship, however informal, with a person outside the nuclear family, and had sustained that relationship over any period of time (regardless of whether it was intact at the time of the interview) was considered for our purposes to have engaged in childwork. One-shot work experiences were, insofar as possible, excluded from such consideration.

We found that the proportion of children with such extra-familial work experiences rose at a very steady pace throughout the elementary years. Among first graders, only 13 percent (26) could legitimately report such experiences. And many of these, while technically acceptable for inclusion, were marginal since they involved social rituals in which the child periodically assisted a neighbor or grandparent in a task such as feeding the cat or bringing in the milk bottles, usually for a nominal fee, such as a penny or a nickel. Nevertheless, as it was clear that these children viewed such tasks as their "jobs," it was decided to include them.

By third grade the number of children who had ever engaged in childwork had risen to about three in eight (39 percent, N=79). Unlike our findings in previous aspects of this study there was no large increase in the participation of fifth graders in such activity: 42 percent (89) of them reported having had such experiences. Fully three-fourths (N=95) of the seventh graders sampled, however, could report childwork.[54] Moreover, about one seventh grader in four (26 percent, N=32) could even report a "work history" of sorts, having had more than one legitimate episode of childwork under the belt. Prior to grade seven, the proportion of youngsters with that level of work experience had been negligible indeed.

This pattern was more general than had been expected, a fact which was no doubt due in some measure to our liberalization of the definition of the term to include employment by neighbors and out-of-household blood relatives. In any event, we found no significant differences in the incidence of childwork by sex, by SES, or by community of residence. Grade in school, at the risk of being repetitious, was associated with the incidence of childwork.

The most commonly reported categories of extra-familial childhood employment were yardwork (mowing lawns, weeding gardens, raking leaves), babysitting, and the delivery of newspapers, in that order. Among children in grades three and five, respectively, 89 percent (70) and 87 percent (83) of those reporting childwork had experience in one or more of these three childhood "occupations." This not only confirms the previous observations of Engel et al. with respect to the restricted range of childwork, it also suggests another. If asked to identify the single most common denominator with regard to childwork, one would do well to specify that it largely involves *interactions with neighbors.* Whose lawn needs mowing? Whose children need minding? Whose need for a newspaper gives employment to many a local child? The obvious answer to these questions suggests that the neighbor serves as "employer of first resort." Indeed we found tht 65 percent (60) of the boys and 70 percent (52) of the girls responding when asked for whom they had logged their initial work experiences said it had been for neighbors or friends of the family, typically by age ten or earlier.[55] Only one child in five reported having *started* extrafamilial work in the employ of a business concern.

None of this should prove particularly surprising. Yet it is worthy of mention, insofar as the social role of the neighbor as employer and/or agent of initiation into the world of work remains largely overlooked in the literature on the sociology of work.[56] Having interviewed neither parents nor neighbors/employers, we can only speculate on the matter. Assuming that parents do value their children's gaining outside work experiences at an early age, each may see in his neighbor the potential to play a role which, however much needs to be done at home, one cannot play for one's own child, namely that of "outside," yet known and trusted "employer." It is not difficult to imagine a set of circumstances under which norms of reciprocity evolve among neighbors regarding the salutory employment of one another's children when the opportunity presents itself. One can conceive even of the occasional "creation" of childwork in order that the social function of introducing the child to the world of work may be carried out early, and in a "safe" environment. This is not to suggest, however, that all childwork, or even most of it, is invented or may be viewed as crumbs brushed aside from the table of adult chores. On the contrary, it is likely that the child labor force plays an important, although neglected, role in the community. It frees adults from certain tasks, enables them to allocate their efforts more efficiently, and in some instances fulfills needs for valuable services (like babysitting or newspaper delivery) which might otherwise go unmet. It is suggested, in any event, that such matters as the role of the neighbor as socializing agent into childwork and the social significance to the local community of the child labor force merit further investigation.

The investigation of children's reports of remuneration for childwork yielded an additional observation. Financial compensation appears to shift with age from ad hoc arrangements to more formal, calculated formulas. Among younger children, the most commonly-reported arrangement was for the child to be paid "by the job." We learned, for example, that first and third graders typically accept *what is given*, often times not knowing how much it will be until the work is completed. This practice is not unlike that of "tipping" service employees, except that it extends to a broader range of activities. Fifth and seventh graders, on the other hand often report *what they charge* for their services, as in the case of $2.50 *per lawn,* or $1.00 *per hour* for babysitting. Note the (relatively) rational nature of such schemes. Many others report performance of regular responsibilities for which they are paid not as the work is done, but on a weekly or bi-weekly basis. It may be that to defer such gratification is thought to be inappropriate for younger children, but that routinization of payments which, after all, approximates the usual practice in the adult world, is regarded as "healthy" for older children. We cannot say. But the pattern of progression toward increasingly abstract schemes of remuneration was nonetheless clearly in evidence.

Adults are often heard to recollect, favorably or otherwise, how they "plunged" into work as children. That metaphor would be inaccurate, to say the least, if applied to the earliest work experiences of the children surveyed here. Clearly the transition to work begins gradually. To set the above metaphor straight, rather than plunging into the labor pool, most of these children reported first dipping their big toes. For almost half, a first "job" meant a commitment of not more than two hours per week.[57] Only one in twelve reported spending in excess of ten hours weekly at his or her initial job. The median category was three to six hours. While such reports did not differ significantly by sex or community of residence, there were minor differences by socioeconomic status. Among children who have worked, middle-class youngsters tended to be somewhat more immersed from the start, i.e., they reported slightly greater time commitments to initial jobs than did working-class pupils.[58]

Naturally, the pattern of earnings at the initial job was in keeping with the modest investments of time. Children's initial work experiences are not only peripheral concerns in terms of time commitments, they also net, in adult terms[59] quite meager returns, as Table 2.20 clearly illustrates. For two-thirds of the children who could recall, first jobs had yielded less than five dollars per week in compensation. Only about one in seven could report weekly earnings in excess of ten dollars.

Earlier in this chapter we reported upon several instances in which it was possible to note "watershed" periods of sorts with regard to children's cognitive development concerning the world of work. The period between grades three and five repeatedly emerged as a time of rapid conceptual development. In the matter of the child's work experiences, seventh grade appears to be a distinctive level in many respects. Regarding the child's actual participation in work, the list of potential barriers includes, among other things, parental wishes,

TABLE 2.20
Recollected earning at first
extrafamilial job*

Less than $1.00 per week	35.7% (83)
$1.00 - $4.99 per week	31.5 (73)
$5.00 - $9.99 per week	19.0 (44)
$10.00 - $19.99 per week	8.6 (20)
$20.00 or more per week	5.2 (12)
Total cases	232

* Percentages are based upon the number of children (N-232 who reported having worked and could recall the amount received for their efforts at "first jobs."

the local opportunity structure, even statutory regulations limiting child labor and establishing criteria for the issuance of working papers. Thus, we cannot conclude on the basis of the evidence presented that seventh graders, say, are more "ready" for the world of work. We can, however, observe that in terms of the degree of their reported participation in the world of work, seventh graders may be considered in a separate category from their younger schoolmates.

Perhaps as good a way as any to make this point would be to construct a "composite" description based upon the information gathered about seventh graders' work experiences. Chances are about three in four, as we have seen above, that our hypothetical seventh grader has at least one genuine episode of childwork in his or her background. In fact, one in three who have worked can report more than one such instance of regular, extrafamilial, paid work involvement, a fact found in virtually none of the work histories of younger children. If our subject were a boy, initial work experiences are likely to have come in the form of yardwork or groundskeeping for neighbors, or delivery of newspapers. If female, babysitting would be the logical guess, once again for neighbors or friends of the family.

Chances are about one in three that our hypothetical child could report having worked for an organization, rather than merely being of assistance to an individual friend or neighbor. (This tends to be more true of boys, some of whom report being called upon by church or civic groups to set up tables for affairs, distribute flyers, etc., not to mention the built-in bias in this direction which exists because newspapers tend to employ boys.) Among children below seventh grade, not a single incident of institutional employment was reported. It is clear that seventh graders, for a number of reasons cited above, have access to a broader work world than do younger children. Moreover their involvement in that world is more extensive. For more than a third of working seventh graders (36 percent, $N=34$), paid work involves a commitment of at least seven hours per week; for one in six (17 percent, $N=16$) it means more than ten hours weekly. Correspondingly, the modal category of weekly earnings among this group rises to between five and ten dollars,[60] while it is no longer uncommon for a child to be earning twenty dollars a week or more.[61] With age and the changes in the child's work and pay situations, the nature of the remunerative process is also likely to differ from that of younger children. Only one in five working children at this level (21 percent, $N=20$) reports being paid under the ad hoc arrangements so typical for younger children. Routinely, pay is calculated—as opposed to bestowed—usually on the basis of a single pre-ordained formula. "My rate," a seventh grader might say, "is one dollar an hour."

All of this is a far cry from the world of work as experienced, for example, by the nine-year-old. Anthropologist Mary Goodman has lamented the fact that modern urban societies provide little in the way of opportunity for real work by children.[62] In our analysis of children's work experiences we have, by and large, found this to be the case. Seventh grade, however, ought to be regarded as perhaps the beginning of a transitional phase in which, in terms of form if not content, the child's work experience undergoes a metamorphosis, emerging with more in common with the adult world of work than that of younger children.

Summary

Alexander Pope, in his *Essay on Man,* long ago declared that "The child is father to the man." The task of determining at what point the child "gives birth," as it were, to a socialized "product" has largely been left to social scientists. In this chapter we have been concerned in particular with the child's cognitive development with respect to work. We have explored a number of issues under that umbrella question. Do we have a pattern to point to for our efforts? The answer would seem to be a qualified yes. The pattern of age-related growth in awareness of work-related phenomena has been apparent throughout our findings thus far. While we have noted, on the one hand, examples of surprisingly high awareness from very early ages and, on the other, a few instances of genuine "threshhold effects," it is nonetheless possible to point to a general pattern of steady cognitive growth throughout the elementary years, with the greatest changes usually coming around grade five.

Such a general observation requires considerable qualification. In the first place, it should be acknowledged that variations by specific items were in some cases quite large. And, there were instances in which other demographic variables, particularly sex and socio-economic status, influenced the results. On the other hand, there were very few cases of no cognitive growth to report despite the great many variables examined here. Moreover, that the pattern is indeed developmental or age-related is attested to by the consistency with which changes in cognition were found to be significantly, and often strongly, related to grade in school, without regard to any existing relationships with other variables. The latter, in any event, were surprisingly few.

Let us turn our attention now to other aspects of the development of children's work orientations, using the general pattern discerned here as a backdrop.

Notes

1. Philippe Aries, *Centuries of Childhood: A Social History of Family Life,* trans. Robert Baldick (New York: Vintage Books, 1965), p. 128.
2. The interviewer presented the situation of a simple cash transaction. Pupils were asked to explain the events which transpired in a way that an alien could follow.
3. Strauss traced concept development with regard to money in Indiana

school children ages four to eleven. See: Anselm L. Strauss, "The Development and Transformation of Monetary Meanings in the Child," *American Sociological Review* 18 (June 1952), pp. 275-286.

4. Danziger's findings are based on interviews with Australian school children ages five to eight. See Kurt Danziger, "Children's Earliest Concepts of Economic Relationships," *Journal of Social Psychology* 57 (May 1958), pp. 231-240.

5. To be more precise, Strauss had suggested that such awareness develops in stages one through four of his schema, meaning by about the age of five. See: Anselm L. Strauss, "Development and Transformation."

6. For purposes of coding, the designation of "personal" uses was reserved for cases in which the child indicated that the salesclerk either kept the money for him/herself or spent it on personal needs. If the child answered literally, i.e., that the money was placed in the cash register (43.8 percent, N=259 said so) the answer was coded as a business exchange. Probing by interviewers among first- and third-grade respondents indicated that receipts were placed in the register temporarily, until the store's owner used them to meet business expenses.

7. The so-called "Don't Know Index" has long been used in studies of childhood socialization as a means of operationalizing the growth of awareness in indirect but quantifiable terms. This does assume, however, that most children not answering "Don't know" do in fact offer reasonably appropriate answers to the question. In this case, that assumption is felt to be warranted.

8. Pupils in grades one, three, and five were asked to explain the concept of work to an "alien." First and third graders were interviewed; fifth graders wrote their answers. Seventh graders answered in writing a similar question phrased more straightforwardly, without the subterfuge of the hypothetical alien.

9. Our findings in general corroborate those of Smith and Proshansky, who had earlier noted sex differences in children's social definitions of work. They had also reported that high school students were more likely than younger children to stress the compulsory nature of work. Indeed our content analyses showed "work-as-obligation" to be the predominant second response of seventh graders, offered by 34 percent (N=15) of those furnishing more than one theme. This was not the case with younger children. See: Robert Smith and Harold Proshansky, *Conceptions of Work, Play, Competence, and Occupation in Junior and Senior High School Students: Final Report* (Ann Arbor, Mich.: University of Michigan, Institute for Social Research, 1967).

10. P.M. Freeston, "Vocational Interests in Elementary School Children," *Occupational Psychology* 13 (July 1939), pp. 223-237.

11. Walter W. Emmerich, "Young Children's Discrimination of Parent and Child Roles," *Child Development* 30 (September 1959), pp. 403-419.

12. Lois B. DeFleur, "Ascending Occupational Knowledge in Young Children," *Sociological Inquiry* 36 (Winter 1966), pp. 98-115.

13. Note that we have been speaking thus far only of children's cognitions

with respect to adulthood. How they *feel* about it is a separate issue, discussion of which is reserved for chapter 4, which deals with affective states.

14. Robert Smith and Harold Proshansky, *Conceptions of Work,* pp. 1-2.

15. Eugene A. Weinstein, "Weights Assigned by Children to Criteria of Prestige," *Sociometry* 19 (June 1956), pp. 126-132.

16. For a list of these occupations, see the Occupational Sorting Task.

17. For a fuller, more precise discussion of the situs dimensions, see: Emile Benoit-Smullyan, "Status, Status Types, and Status Interrelations," *American Sociological Review* 9 (April 1944), pp. 154-161. See also: Richard T. Morris and Raymond J. Murphy, "The Situs Dimension of Occupational Structure," *American Sociological Review* 24 (April 1959), pp. 231-239.

18. Throughout this report all respondents' names, indeed all proper nouns have been changed to preserve the anonymity of the pupils involved and their families. Also, in some cases, probe questions were inserted by the interviewer in order to get children to elaborate on matters under discussion. For purposes of clarity and simplicity probe questions are omitted wherever this practice does no damage to the substance of the child's answer.

19. Seventh graders answered the same question in writing as did fifth graders, but on the Knowledge of Work Questionnaire, Part II.

20. Eli Ginzberg et al., *Occupational Choice* (New York: Columbia University Press, 1951).

21. Sociologists have long been divided on this issue, falling roughly into two camps: Those who believe that differential rewards are offered to enhance the attractiveness of certain lines to work which are "functionally important" to society, and those who reject this explanation, often in favor of a conflict-oriented alternative. For a discussion of the seminal issues involved here, see: Kingsly Davis and Wilbert E. Moore, "Some Principles of Stratification," *American Sociological Review* 10 (April 1945), pp. 242-249. See also a critique of this position by: Melvin M. Tumin, "Some Principles of Stratification: A Critical Analysis," *American Sociological Review* 18 (August 1953), pp. 387-393.

22. The child's idealization of political authority figures prominently in several studies of political socialization. For a review of this literature, see: Fred I. Greenstein, *Children and Politics* (New Haven, Conn.: Yale University Press, 1969), pp. 31-54. See also: Fred I. Greenstein, "The Benevolent Leader: Children's Images of Political Authority," *American Political Science Review* 14 (December 1960), pp. 934-943. For consideration of how such imagery is thought to translate into attachment to a political system, see: Robert D. Hess and Judith V. Torney, *The Development of Political Attitudes,* especially chapters 2 and 3.

23. Edward S. Greenberg, "Orientations of Black and White Children to Political Authority Figures," *Social Science Quarterly* 51 (December 1970), pp. 561-571.

24. Danziger, in his 1958 study of Australian school children, had noted a similar shift from the purely social to the economic in children's conceptualizations of the role of the boss. He, however, was able to discern

this shift by age eight, the oldest level at which he tested. Here the shift comes somewhat later. See Kurt Danziger, "Children's Earliest Concepts."

25.   Children in grades one, three, and five were asked to explain the term "boss" to a hypothetical alien. Seventh graders were asked to explain what was involved in being a boss.

26.   Kurt Danziger, "Children's Earliest Concepts."

27.   Mason Haire and Florence Morrison, "School Children's Perceptions of Labor and Management," *Journal of Social Psychology* 44 (November 1957), pp. 179-197.

28.   Mason Haire and Florence Morrison, "School Children's Perceptions," p. 189.

29.   Mason Haire and Florence Morrison, "School Children's Perceptions."

30.   Specifically, the actual responses of the third and fifth graders were distributed as follows. Thirty percent of respondents from middle class families (N=21) as compared to 50 percent of respondents from working class families (N=74) thought strikes are right; 28 percent of both groups (N=17 and 41) thought strikes were wrong; and 39 percent (N=23) of the former and 22 percent (N=32) of the latter gave conditional responses (X^2=6.81, p < .05).

31.   First graders are not included in Table 2.11 since only ten both recognized the strike situation as a labor dispute and had formulated opinions on the matter.

32.   Among seventh graders, 58 percent (42) of the boys said strikes were right, compared to 35 percent (19) of the girls. On the other hand, 37 percent (20) of seventh grade girls answered conditionally, versus only 18 percent (13) boys. (X^2=7.985, p < .05).

33.   Here the standard applied in classifying children's responses as correct was rather liberal indeed. Any child who identified welfare as money for the poor or for those *unable* to work, and/or as a situation in which the government pays for the living expenses of the poor, was considered to have at least a functional understanding of the concept.

34.   Children in grades one, three, and five were asked to explain the concept of welfare to the alien, who had supposedly overheard two men arguing over whether the practice was right or wrong. Fifth graders answered in writing. Younger children were interviewed. Seventh graders were asked to define welfare in writing, and to evaluate it.

35.   Among seventh graders 51 percent (22) of those from middle class backgrounds correctly identified welfare, compared to 71 percent (29) of those of working class backgrounds. (X^2=2.9, p=ns).

36.   Robert J. Havighurst, "Youth in Exploration and Man Emergent," in *Man in a World at Work,* ed. Henry Borow (Boston: Houghton-Mifflin, 1964), p. 223.

37.   "Identification with a worker" was the first of six vocational developmental tasks specified by Havighurst. It was to encompass roughly the age bracket from five to ten years of age. See: Robert J. Havighurst, "Youth in Exploration," pp. 215 ff.

38.   For a more general theoretical dimension of the process of identification with parents, see: Albert Bandura, "Social Learning Theory of Identifi-

catory Processes," in *Handbook of Socialization Theory and Research,* ed. David A. Goslin (Chicago: Rand-McNally, 1969), pp. 213-262. For examples of specific applications of role modeling theory to vocational development, see: John O. Crites, "Parental Identification in Relation to Vocational Interest Development," *Journal of Educational Psychology* 53 (December 1962), pp. 262-270; George M. Appleton and James C. Hanson, "Parent Child Relations, Need Nurturance, and Vocational Orientation," *Personnel and Guidance Journal* 47 (1969), pp. 794-799; William G. Dyer, "Parental Influence on the Job Attitudes of Children from Two Occupational Strata," *Sociology and Social Research* 42 (January-February 1958), pp. 203-206.

39.   This depth of information scale does not purport to test the accuracy of pupils' accounts of parental work activities, merely the detail of same. Nor can we claim to know the degree to which such a technique is biased in favor of more verbal children. Scoring was conducted as follows: one point for knowing whether the parent worked; one point each for knowing the department, the name of the company, and the town in which it is located; up to three points, depending upon specificity, for furnishing job title; up to two points for furnishing a rationale for the job; and up to four points for description of the tasks involved in the work.

40.   Sex role identification has occupied a prominent position in consideration of the socialization process since Freud. For some sociological treatments of the process, see: Lawrence A. Kohlberg, "A Cognitive-Developmental Analysis of Children's Sex-Role Concepts and Attitudes," in *The Development of Sex Differences,* ed. Eleanor Maccoby (Stanford, Calif.: Stanford University Press, 1966). See also Talcott Parsons and Robert F. Bales, eds., *Family, Socialization, and Interaction Process* (Glencoe, Ill: Free Press, 1955).

41.   William C. Dyer, "Parental Influence."

42.   Hartley has noted the existence of special sex-role pressures facing male children due in part to relative inaccessibility of male role models. See: Ruth E. Hartley, "Sex-Role Pressures and the Socialization of the Male Child," *Psychological Reports* 5 (September 1959), pp. 457-468. Similarly, Biber et al., "Feminization in Preschool," *Developmental Psychology* 7 (July 1972), p. 86.

43.   Here, "higher" levels refers to categories 1 and 2 (professional/ managerial) and "working class" levels refers to categories 5, 6, and 7 in the Hollingshead occupational schema. See: August B. Hollingshead, "A Two-Factor Index of Social Position," (Unpublished mimeographed paper, 1957).

44.   Helene R. Marshall and Lucille V. Magruder, "Relation Between Parent Money Education Practices and Children's Knowledge and Use of Money," *Child Development* 31 (June 1960), pp. 253-284.

45.   The lone difference by community was in Exeter, the most affluent of the towns involved. Predictably, a slightly higher proportion of children in this town (63.6 percent, N=131) received allowances than in other towns (56.6 percent, N=313). ($X^2 = 17.51$, $p < .01$). Similarly, there were slight, but not statistically significant differences by SES, with 64 percent of middle class children (N=288) of working class children.

46. Among middle class children 80 percent (161) report having regular chores compared to 87 percent (440) of working class children. $(X^2 = 11.21, p < .01)$.

47. These are of course rhetorical questions, to which one might answer that the percentages under discussion are based on children's *reports* of their chores rather than upon observations of actual behavior.

48. Robert J. Havighurst, "Youth in Exploration," pp. 216-222.

49. Underlying all of this concern, of course, is the often unstated assumption that performance of routine tasks is associated with the development of responsibility in children. Dale B. Harris et al. investigated this hypothesis in a survey of 3,000 school children in the early 1950s, however, without producing any strong evidence to suggest the existence of such a relationship. See: Dale B. Harris et al., "The Relationship of Children's Home Duties to Responsibility," *Child Development* 25 (March 1954), pp. 29-33.

50. The percentages of children reporting occasional performance of "special jobs" in addition to regular chores are as follows: first grade, 70 percent (161); third grade, 87 percent (177); fifth grade, 80 percent (171); seventh grade, 92 percent (121).

51. Mary Engel et al., "Orientation to Work in Children," American *Journal of Orthopsychiatry* 38 (January 1968), pp. 137-143.

52. The other three precipitants of occupational choice as named by Borow were (1) courses of study and the institutional pressure brought by schools to make "branching decisions," (2) parents, and (3) "other significant persons." See: Henry Borow, "Development of Occupational Motives and Roles," in *Review of Child Development Research*, ed. Lois W. Hoffman and Martin L. Hoffman (New York: Russell Sage Foundation, 1966), pp. 373-423.

53. For a fuller discussion of what is involved in this concept of "work style," and its significance, see: Mary Engel et al., "Children Who Work and the Concept of Work Style," *Psychiatry* 30 (November 1967), pp. 392-404.

54. Engel et al. had reported a 73 percent incidence of childwork among children in grades four to eight in three SES groups from Metropolitan Boston in the mid-1960's. See: Engel et al, "Orientation to Work." Sorenson and Morris had found that 73 percent of the males and 69 percent of the females in a study of ninth graders in Los Angeles reported having worked, mostly in areas of babysitting, paper routes, and yardwork. See: A.G. Sorenson and Irma E. Morris, "Attitudes and Beliefs as Sources of Vocational Preference," *Journal of Educational Research* 56 (September 1962), pp. 20-27.

55. Insofar as *when* they started work was concerned, three children in four (76 percent, N=198) who could recall said they had started by age ten. More accurately, 14 percent (35) report starting by age six, 32 percent (83) at age seven or eight, 31 percent (80) at age nine or ten, and 24 percent (62) at age eleven or twelve.

56. Probably the most informative discussion on the social role of the neighbor is Suzanne Keller's, but it does not mention the significance of neighbors in child vocational development. See: Suzanne Keller, *The

Urban Neighborhood: A Sociological Perspective, (New York: Random House, 1968), esp. pp. 19-86.

57. Among children claiming to recall the amount of time usually spent at first extrafamilial job, 47 percent (95) reported spending not more than two hours per week, 33 percent (68) three to six hours, 11 percent (23) seven to ten hours, and 8 percent (18) more than ten hours.

58. The SES differences in question here are most clearly visible when the data are collapsed as follows:

Time Spent Weekly, Initial Job:	Middle Class	Working Class
Two hours or less	33.8%	53.1%
	(22)	(68)
Three to ten hours	39.3	41.4
	(32)	(53)
More than ten hours	16.9	5.5
	(11)	(7)
Total cases	65	128

$(X^2 = 10.1 \qquad p. < .01)$

59. Adult standards are, of course, exactly the *wrong* ones to employ if one hopes to understand the meaning such compensation holds for children. The relativity of such matters was amply illustrated by Engel and her colleagues in their discussion of the case of "Ralph," their prototypical "working boy." At age ten, fifty cents a day satisfied Ralph for his efforts shining shoes. Even when the older boys told him that was not so good, he replied that it was for him. By age thirteen, however, Ralph was not satisfied with himself unless he had earned five dollars a day. See: Mary Engel et al., "Children Who Work."

60. This compares favorably with the mean weekly earnings of $5.43 reported by children in grades four to eight in the Boston area in the 1960s. See: Mary Engel, et al., "Orientations to Work."

61. To be more precise, among the 95 working seventh graders, 28 percent (27), reported earning less than $5.00 per week, 37 percent (35) between $5.00 and $9.99, 17 percent (16), between $10.00 and $19.99, and 18 percent (17) more than $20.00 per week.

62. Mary Ellen Goodman, *The Culture of Childhood: Child's Eye View of Society and Culture* (New York: Teachers College Press, 1970), esp. ch. 5.

Chapter 3

The Protestant Ethic and the
Spirit of Childhood

In keeping with the long-standing annual presidential tradition, Richard Nixon declared confidently that "America's competitive spirit, the 'work ethic' of this people, is alive and well on Labor Day, 1971."[1] That his administration, along with many other Americans, harbored some doubts on the matter could be inferred less than four months later when the Secretary of Health, Education, and Welfare Elliot L. Richardson commissioned a special task force to study work in America.[2] One major question before the commission concerned the fate of the work ethic in America in recent years. Speculation as to the death of the Protestant ethic, even its possible replacement by a "no-work ethic," had become a favorite pastime of the media[3] as well as the academic, business and labor communities.[4] For such questions to be raised at all in the land which had long celebrated the aphorisms of Ben Franklin and given such credence to the Horatio Alger myth was indeed an interesting development.

Our present interest in such matters derives from the fact that one aspect of children's orientations has to do with their attachment to work. While many writers have stressed that today's young workers are challenging the work ethic, the evidence of such a trend is far from compelling.[5] Nor is there any research suggesting whether such an alleged decline in attachment to the work ethic, if it exists at all, might be attributed to some "failure" in the process of socialization to work or is perhaps the result of workers' reactions to contemporary structural or organizational conditions. In order to shed light on this issue, we shall in this chapter consider the work ethic as it is manifest during childhood.

Doing so requires that we operationalize the concept of the work ethic in a way that permits us to explore its status during childhood. There are at least two lines along which we might proceed. We could define the work ethic behaviorally, as Ivar Berg has done, using as indicants of commitment such factors as thrift, diligence, level of craftsmanship, and the inclination to defer gratification.[6] This approach has its merits, to be sure, and might in fact have proven ideal were we dealing with a sample of working adults whose daily occupational activities were subject to long-term observation. Our subjects in the present investigation, however, are children whose work experiences are limited and hardly comparable to those of adults. Moreover, our data consist not of observations but of self-reports and responses to survey items. Clearly, we shall want to operationalize the concept of the Protestant ethic by emphasizing its cognitive-attitudinal aspects, which is in keeping with Weber's original use of the term.[7] For what Weber had in mind was on the one hand an attitude set and on the other a prevailing cultural definition of work stressing its ontological and spiritual significance. This is not to suggest that work must be viewed as having formal religious significance per se. Indeed, one of Weber's principal theses was that this world-view which had its roots in early Protestantism had broadened and become secularized, that it was a dominant cultural theme which attaches a positive moral connotation to work. Such an orientation involves cognitive factors: the perception of work as a "calling" or "duty," and the tendency to define frugality or the accumulation of economic rewards as indicants of personal worth. It also involves evaluative factors: the imputation of moral significance to hard work, the deprecation of idleness, or the tendency to attach high priority to success and achievement.

Robin Williams, in identifying what he called the "dominant value configurations" in American society, stressed several manifestations of the significance of the work ethic in our culture. He noted the tendencies of Americans to equate occupational achievement with personal excellence, and to define "success" largely in terms of economic rewards. Yet he noted, too, our cultural predisposition to evaluate success highly, but only within a certain ethical framework based upon fair play and the like. Much of this transpires, he suggested, at the symbolic level. Money, for example, is often valued not merely for what it will buy, but as a sign of personal success. Similarly, the American love for business may be interpreted along these lines, i.e., "bigger" equals "better" to many of us. Ours is a culture, he observed, which places great stock in action and mastery of the physical world, and which has elevated efficiency and practicality to the level of virtues. Moreover, he contended, we are a nation of moralizers: We do not merely observe; we pass judgments at every opportunity, imposing the application of ethical principles upon matters which in other cultures would not be subject to such tests.[8]

If we assume a fair amount of truth in Williams' characterization of our culture, we may state our purpose in this chapter quite succinctly. We are concerned with a single question, namely the issue of how fully our children share these dominant work-related values and perceptions. We shall devote our attention therefore to consideration of a number of lesser issues which, taken together, may shed some light on the status of the work ethic during childhood. Our observations will be organized around three central themes: (1) children's evaluation of work, (2) their aspirations, and (3) their savings habits.

Children's Evaluation of Work

The social history of this nation can hardly be told without reference to the work ethic, our preeminant social doctrine and guiding myth. From the seventeenth-century New England pietism of Cotton Mather to the exhortations of Norman Vincent Peale, work has had strong religious legitimations and significance. In between, countless secular proponents—from Benjamin Franklin to Andrew Carnegie, from P.T. Barnum to Horatio Alger—have variously attributed to work a moral significance that is perhaps peculiarly American. Franklin's *Poor Richard's Almanac* celebrated diligence and thrift above all else. Alger's rags-to-riches tales were said to have had a readership of some fifty million during his lifetime.[9] In order to ascertain the degree to which the work ethic is internalized by children in our own day, we asked our respondents several questions designed to elicit information on their evaluation of work.

Work is defined by children as activity undertaken principally to obtain money. Many also report regular earning experiences. But do they perceive any intrinsic merit in working? Or do they merely see work as a means to an end? In order to explore the status of the work ethic during childhood, we asked children to tell us whether they would work if pay were not an issue, that is, if they had no need for the money. The answer was a rather resounding yes; about three of four children indicated they would do so. This varied little by grade, except that conditional answers, as usual, became more manifest in seventh grade.

Lest the reader be lead to any premature conclusions, it is important to qualify these findings. The reason most frequently offered by those children who indicated they would work even if they did not need the money was a desire for "extra money." Almost half of the children giving reasons cited the desire for more money, which many said they would "save for a rainy day" or use to buy items they could not otherwise afford. About one child in five indicated either liking work in general or enjoyment of a specific task; 12.5 percent (46) mentioned the desire to keep occupied, while 11 percent (40) said they would work for the sake of being helpful.

These reasons varied somewhat depending upon the age of the children. The desire for extra money apparently becomes slightly more prominent with age, while the "like to work" response, which was not dominant to begin with, diminishes considerably after grade one.[10] Sex differences, while relatively small, center upon two predictable categories: boys were slightly more money-oriented, whereas girls were more likely to indicate the desire to be helpful.[11] Socioeconomic status and community of residence were not significantly related to children's responses on this matter.

Only a relatively small portion of the children queried (17 percent, $N=89$) offered reasons for their assertions that they would not work unless they needed the money. About half of these said, in effect, that money was the sole *raison d'etre* for working—i.e., that apart from the need for money, they saw no point to working. There was no pattern to the remainder of the negative responses, nor were the children who offered them disproportionately distributed by grade, sex, SES, or community.

We must reserve our discussion of the significance of these findings until we have examined other material to be presented shortly. However, two fundamental observations based upon the evidence above are worthy of mention. For one thing, we can state flatly that we found nothing in the responses of these children which points to the existence of any "anti-work" ethic. On the other hand, we would stop short of characterizing most of these pupils' orientations as "pro-work," for it is equally clear that a great many of them are more concerned with monetary rewards than with any intrinsic satisfaction derived from work per se. If this seems like equivocation, so be it. More clearcut conclusions as to the nature and extent of children's commitment to the work ethic must await further consideration of these data.

TABLE 3.1
Expressed preference for challenging work
by grade in school

	Grade in school		
Preference for challenge:	3rd	5th	7th
Low (0-1 point)	70.3%	65.4%	50.8%
	(130)	(138)	(62)
Moderate to high	29.7	34.6	49.2
(2-4 points)	(55)	(73)	(60)
Total cases	185	211	122

$$(x^2 = 12.47 \qquad p<.01)$$

The work ethic extends far beyond mere willingness to work. It includes also a variety of more subtle traits, such as the desire for mastery and control of the work situation[12] and the positive evaluation of challenge. In an effort to assess children's orientations with regard to such matters, we constructed a "challenge index" comprised of four test items. Children in grades three, five, and seven were asked to choose between alternative ways of completing the sentence "The kind of job I would like is . . ." Expressed preferences to be one's own source of occupational control, to work independently, to be pressed to the limit of one's abilities, and to have "final say" over one's work were taken as indicants of positive orientations toward challenge.[13] (Scores on this scale could range from zero to four.) As Table 3.1 shows, the tendency to favorably evaluate challenge is far from pronounced in these children. Among third graders, low scores outnumbered moderate to high scores on this scale by a margin of more than two to one. Thereafter, we note a steady but modest age-related trend in the direction of increasing preference for challenge. By seventh grade about half the respondents opted for at least two of the four challenge-related choices.[14]

The sex differences observed with regard to children's orientations toward challenging work were substantial. In general, 45 percent (124) of the boys scored in the "moderate to high" range, compared to only 26 percent (64) of the girls. Moreover, as Table 3.2 shows, such sex differences increase with age, as boys apparently advance more rapidly than girls in terms of growth in this area. By seventh grade, two-thirds of the boys achieve at least moderate scores, whereas about two-thirds of the girls continue to score low.

TABLE 3.2
Expressed preference for challenging work
by grade and sex

Preference for challenge:	Boys			Girls		
	3rd	5th	7th	3rd	5th	7th
Low (0-1 point)	62% (48)	53% (47)	32% (17)	77% (41)	77% (72)	65% (32)
Moderate to high (2-4 points)	38 (29)	47 (41)	68 (37)	23 (12)	23 (22)	35 (17)
Total cases:	77	88	54	53	94	49

Our interpretation of such differences is that preference for challenge in merely a specific manifestation of aggressiveness in general, a trait commonly believed to be differentially distributed by sex. One might generalize therefore that boys are more aggressive in their work orientations than girls, and that such differentials increase with age during the elementary school years.

It is of interest that Maccoby had found middle-class boys' preferences for positions of authority and responsibility greater than those of working-class boys.[15] Indeed, when controlling here for sex by SES, we did note small but significant differences in this direction, with middle-class boys scoring somewhat higher with respect to their preference to challenging work. SES, however, was not significantly related to such preferences among the girls.

One final observation seems in order with respect to children's evaluation of work. It centers principally upon something children typically did not say, although they had opportunity. A corollary to the tendency to evaluate work highly is of course the inclination to deprecate idleness. "Idle hands," as the old Calvinist maxim states, "are the devil's workshop." Yet this theme proved conspicuously absent with respect to children's assessments of one of the principal categories of non-workers in our society—welfare recipients. In adult society, including the realm of national politics, it is not uncommon to hear welfare programs attacked on grounds that they reward indolence or undermine the incentive to work. As we have seen in the previous chapter, however, children do not seem to attach any moral connotations to poverty, nor do they seem to stigmatize recipients in general. Instead, they typically refer to welfare recipients not as those who *will not* work, but as those who *cannot* work.

Such a perception is of course largely accurate. Thus, the observation that children define welfare recipients, in effect, as "deserving poor" does not necessarily imply anything about the degree to which they have internalized the work ethic. Our argument here is based upon "negative evidence," i.e., upon attributing significance to the fact that children's assessments of welfare did *not* include a variety of moral connotations, such as the imputation of laziness, which we would expect among adults of the same socioeconomic backgrounds as these children.[16]

Several arguments might be offered in rebuttal. First, children may employ selective perceptions. That is they may simply equate not working with inability to do so, giving little or no consideration to the issue of willingness to work. Or, they may sense it is "inappropriate" for them to make such characterizations of welfare recipients, and consequently refrain from giving such answers in interviews or on surveys. Even if either of these two rejoinders proved true, however, our basic contention would remain unchanged. For would not children's failure to mention desire to work or to verbalize negative assessments of non-workers indicate that their commitment to the work ethic was, at best, incomplete? Put differently, assuming these children were fully inculcated with the Protestant ethic, what would be the odds that practically none of them, when asked directly for an opinion regarding welfare, would volunteer any form of deprecation of idleness? Yet this was exactly the case. If this aspect of the work ethic has been internalized by children, we have no evidence of it here.

Our findings with respect to children's evaluation of work are therefore mixed. On the other hand, most report they would work even if they had no need for money. But many say so not because of any satisfaction they expect to derive from working, but because of the desire to accumulate money. This last point can hardly be considered to run counter to the work ethic, merely to indicate a less than perfect version of it. With age, children, especially boys, look more favorably upon the challenge factor, but not to the degree to which we might call them enthusiastic. Finally, children do not openly perceive non-working as idleness, nor do they seem especially prone to view such matters in moralistic terms.

Children's Aspirations

How fully is the American Dream internalized during childhood? The desire to "make something of ourselves," an ideal usually measured in terms of occupational mobility, has long occupied a central position in the American value system. Thereafter (or failing that) we take satisfaction in the success of our children. Great expectations are communicated to children in a variety of forms, including the ubiquitous my-son-the-doctor scenario. The resultant need to achieve is often so pervasive that Studs Terkel, among others, has gone so far as to maintain that the real tragedy of the Great Depression was not so much economic as psychological deprivation, not so much poverty as guilt:[17]

> The suddenly-idle hands blamed themselves, rather than society. True, there were hunger marches and protestations to City Hall and Washington, but the millions experienced a private kind of shame when the pink slip came. No matter that others suffered the same fate, the inner voice whispered "I'm a failure." . . . Outside forces, except to the more articulate and political rebels, were in some vague way responsible, but not really. It was a personal guilt.

No investigation of children's commitment to the work ethic would therefore be complete without considering the extent of children's aspirations toward upward occupational mobility. This necessarily forces us to refer in passing to the phenomenon of stated occupational choice, if only because "aspirations" have meaning only in relative terms. That is to say, without comparing a child's preference with actual parental occupational levels we have no means of classifying him/her as ambitious or otherwise.

It is not our intention here to focus at length on children's occupational choices. For one thing, there is no dearth in the educational literature in this regard.[18] More importantly, however, there are a number of reasons to be skeptical of the fruitfulness of investigating the career choices of elementary children. Ginzberg and his associates have suggested, for example, that occupational decision-making involves a long-term process of "foreclosure," during which alternatives are successively ruled out as the individual gradually gives more weight to interests, capacities, and reality factors.[19] Early in the process, children are necessarily tentative and unrealistic, making it unwise to place much stock in their stated preferences. Moreover, as Super has pointed out, there is reason to believe that vocational preferences, even among high school students, are unstable and transient.[20]

In this section, therefore, our interests in children's stated occupational choices will be restricted to their utility in assessing children's ambitions or mobility aspirations.[21] That is to say, we shall be relatively unconcerned with the precise natures of children's choices, concentrating instead upon the relative social status they are projecting in comparison to their parents.

Let us begin by describing the distribution of stated choices, broken down by social status, for a subsample of children (N=458) who furnished both codable occupational choices and codable information on their fathers' occupations. Table 3.3 presents these preferences of boys and girls in this subsample. These sex differences are quite traditional. Boys were overrepresented among those stating preferences for the major professions (mostly medicine and law) and skilled manual labor (carpentry, mechanics, etc.), and girls disproportionately chose the so-called lesser professions (teaching and nursing). Perhaps surprisingly, few girls projected themselves into clerical/ sales roles, probably due to the popularity of the aforementioned professional positions. Controlling for sex and SES, we found relatively few major changes. Middle-class boys (38.5 percent, N=20) were more likely than working-class boys (20 percent, N=27) to aspire to the major professions or executive positions. On the other hand, 41 percent (54) of boys of working-class background expressed preferences for skilled manual occupations, compared to 29 percent (15) of middle-class boys. Among girls, no SES differences of any consequence were found.

In a departure from previous patterns, grade in school was not significantly related to the status of children's projections, unless sex was controlled. Only when the list of children's choices was collapsed did any meaningful pattern emerge. As Table 3.4 shows, with age boys' projections tended in general to rise, whereas there was evidence of a decline in status projections among the girls. While we have no data on children's feedback from parents and significant others on such matters, these findings do in general support the contention that boys receive more positive reinforcement or nurturance than do girls with respect to professional occupational choices.

TABLE 3.3
Social status of child's occupational choice
by sex

Status of choice:	Boys	Girls
Higher executives, major professionals	25.9% (69)	14.6% (28)
Business managers, lesser professionals	7.9 (21)	45.8 (88)
Administrators, small business owners, lesser professionals	25.9 (69)	18.2 (35)
Clerical, retail, technical workers	1.1 (3)	6.3 (12)
Skilled manual workers	32.0 (85)	10.4 (20)
Machine operators, semi skilled workers	6.4 (17)	4.2 (8)
Unskilled workers	0.8 (2)	0.5 (1)
Total cases:	266	192

$(x^2=109.75$ $p<.001)$

Many of the choices of younger boys, especially first graders, fit under the heading of glamorous and adventurous occupations, just as Lambert and Klineberg had found in their cross-cultural study of the career choices of boys ages six to fourteen.[22] The subsequent shifts do indeed support their interpretation, namely that of a progressive trend from more adventurous choices (fireman, policeman, soldier, etc.) toward more sober and mature choices. Other interpretations are also possible, however. The observed shift from blue-collar to white-collar choices could indicate that status or mobility factors play a greater role in older boys' occupational choices. Or, it could mean simply that young children find it much easier to identify with the more tangible, visible working-class occupations than with white-collar jobs which are, after all, more abstract and less obvious in terms of their importance to the community. For example, a young boy may grasp the nature and significance of the role of police officer far more readily than he might that of insurance salesman. The net result, a greater tendency among younger children to project themselves into roles in the former category, should not surprise us.

TABLE 3.4
Status projections of children's occupational choices by grade and sex

Status levels of choices: (collapsed)	Boys				Girls			
	1st	3rd	5th	7th	1st	3rd	5th	7th
Professional/ managerial	26% (21)	31% (27)	39% (22)	48% (20)	71% (37)	76% (41)	51% (28)	32% (10)
Other white collar	10 (8)	32 (28)	45 (25)	26 (11)	17 (9)	18 (10)	25 (14)	45 (14)
Working class	64 (51)	37 (33)	16 (9)	26 (11)	12 (6)	6 (3)	24 (13)	23 (7)
Total cases:	80	88	56	42	52	54	55	31

Among girls the shift is downward, with (teacher/nurse) professional choices yielding with age to nonprofessional white-collar choices, especially those of secretary-typist and airline hostess. Here, it is not so easy to accept the same explanation as offered above for the shift in the distribution of boys' choices. While teachers and nurses may, by virtue of their positions in the school and community at large, be somewhat more visible as role models to young girls, it would be difficult to consider the roles of secretaries or airline hostesses in our culture as hidden from children, or more abstract, or less glamorous. Nor can we ignore the status dimension. With age, girls' choices clearly decline in terms of the occupational status they are projecting. Given the existence of a reverse trend among boys, we cannot dismiss the possibility of sex-related differentials in the nature of encouragement, suggestions, and reinforcement received by children with respect to their occupational choices. The situation is fraught with potential for self-fulfilling prophecy.[23]

Turning to the issue of children's aspirations or ambitions, it is necessary to consider the relative standings of children's projections versus their reports of actual parental occupations. Following the procedures of Lambert and Klineberg, we constructed "aspiration indices" for classifying children's occupational choices as projecting upward mobility, occupational inheritance,[24] or downward mobility. All the children in this subsample (N=458) were classified in terms of their aspirations vis-a-vis their father's occupational levels. In addition, we have computed children's aspirations relative to the mothers' occupations in cases where there was sufficient information to permit this (N=300).

Since intergenerational occupational mobility is ordinarily figured on the basis of children's status in relation to that of their fathers, we begin our consideration of children's aspirations along these lines. The children in this subsample must be considered *relatively* oriented toward upward mobility. In general, 58 percent (265) aspired to positions on the Hollingshead Scale at least one level above those reportedly occupied by their fathers. The trend was far from overwhelming, however, as the remainder were about equally divided among children projecting no change in status (22 percent, N=101), and those whose choices fell below their fathers' levels in the occupational hierarchy (20 percent, N=92). Girls were in general more likely to have aspirations for upward mobility than boys (70 percent, N=135) compared to (49 percent, N=130), a likely artifact of girls' widespread preferences for the semi-professions, teaching and nursing. Working-class children, as could be expected, were more likely than middle-class children to aspire to move upward (63 percent, N=100) compared to (44 percent, N=48), if only because in our index aspirations are a function of the relatively low status levels of their fathers' jobs.

It is only when these aspirational levels are examined by grade and sex together that we begin to perceive any meaningful pattern. As Table 3.5 clearly reveals, the same general age-sex-related trend obtains with respect to aspirations as was observed above regarding children's choices. That is to say, boys' occupational projections steadily become more ambitious with age, whereas those of girls (although higher than those of boys in large part due to the initial popularity of the nurse and teacher choices) do not. Indeed by grade seven, there are indications that girls' ambitions are on the decline.

Naturally, since many working mothers occupy positions of lower status than their husbands, we should not be surprised to learn that children's aspirations are uniformly higher relative to their mothers' occupations than they were versus those of their fathers. Nearly four out of five children of working mothers in this subsample (78 percent,

N=233) projected themselves at occupational levels above those of their mothers. Neither age nor sex nor SES nor community of residence made even the slightest difference in the extent of children's tendencies to aspire to occupational levels above those of their mothers. Grade in school proved significantly related to such aspira-

TABLE 3.5
Children's aspirations relative to
fathers' occupational status
by grade and sex

Occupational level aspired to:	Boys				Girls			
	1st	3rd	5th	7th	1st	3rd	5th	7th
Higher than father's	39%	44%	59%	64%	69%	80%	69%	58%
	(31)	(39)	(33)	(27)	(36)	(43)	(38)	(18)
Same as father's	36	36	20	14	10	11	16	10
	(29)	(32)	(11)	(6)	(5)	(6)	(9)	(3)
Lower than father's	25	19	21	21	21	9	15	32
	(20)	(17)	(12)	(9)	(11)	(5)	(8)	(10)
Total cases:	80	88	56	42	52	54	55	31

tions only when controlling for sex. Among boys, there was an age-related trend of increasing mobility projections vis-a-vis maternal occupational levels which was not the least bit in evidence among the girls. The proportion of boys indicating such upward aspirations rose from 70 percent (30) among first graders to 93.5 percent (29) among seventh graders in this subsample.

What can be said in summary of our analysis of children's expressed levels of ambition? First, we might reiterate that upward mobility aspirations were clearly, but not universally, in evidence among these children. To that we would add the observation that such ambitions, while in general widespread, are not distributed at random among these children. Predictably, socioeconomic status was associated with differences in children's aspirations, especially with regard to professional and skilled manual occupations. Age and sex, in tandem, made for differential patterns of mobility aspirations. Phrased in developmental terms, boys appear to *grow into* ambitions, whereas girls show slight signs of *outgrowing* their earlier high level ambitions by about grade seven.

Children's Savings Habits

The real contribution of Max Weber's important thesis, *The Protestant Ethic and the Spirit of Capitalism,* lay not so much in the accuracy of his characterization of a certain dominant value configuration in Western civilization as in the fact that he went beyond that. He asserted that it was no mere coincidence that Protestantism and capitalism should emerge (in that order) from the civilizations of Western Europe, that the pervasiveness of the former contributed significantly to the creation of a propitious value climate for the rise of the latter. The defining structural characteristic which sets capitalism apart from all other business arrangements, according to Weber, was the systematic, rational calculation of all profits in terms of capital acquisition which both increments the net worth of the establishment and, more importantly, improves its basis for continuous renewal of profits.[25]

At the individual level, corresponding in many respects to capitalism at the organizational level, there occurred what Weber termed "the limitation of consumption" and "the release of acquisitive activity" which combined to produce an "ascetic compulsion to save."[26] Here we will take up the question of children's savings habits, not because we see in them any indications of asceticism or the like, but merely because such information may lead to inferences about the degree to which children internalize the work ethic. In short, we shall assume the tendency to save money to be indicative, in some small way at least, of the child's inculcation with the ethos we have been discussing.

Earlier, we have noted that many children cited the desire for "extra money" as the reason for their stated willingness to work, whether or not they needed the money. Now, in considering children's savings habits, we are again tapping the same dimension of their work orientations. But which dimension is it? We offer two principal candidates: acquisitiveness and/or the inclination to defer gratification. Let us examine their responses for clues.

In recognition of the simplistic versions of certain money-related behaviors among children,[27] we have defined "savings" in the broadest possible sense of the term. Thus, we allow for the existence of a dichotomy in children's saving habits—some go the piggy-bank route, others use commercial banks. The overwhelming majority of children asked (82 percent, N=544) reported saving money in one fashion or another. There is, however, an apparent decline in the incidence of saving among older children. Since fifth and seventh graders were surveyed in writing whereas younger children were interviewed, we are inclined to view this decline as an artifact of the lack of probe questions at the higher grade levels. But we cannot rule out that such a trend actually takes place among older children who, after all, have more opportunity to spend their money and, presumably, more complex wants than younger children. In any event, it is nonetheless quite clear that most children sampled report saving money from as early as grade one.

No significant differences by sex, SES, or community of residence were found in children's reports of their general savings habits.

In most instances of children's reports of saving activities (71 percent, N=388) further information was obtained concerning how the child saved money. In general, the number of children reporting saving at home (60 percent, N=231) was approximately equal to that of children reporting utilization of commercial or savings banks (55 percent, N=214), with a few (15 percent, N=57) reporting both practices. When these responses are controlled by grade in school, however, a clear pattern emerges. As Table 3.6 suggests, the majority of children who report saving money (and most do) are apparently initiated into the practice in the home, through "piggy bank" or "coffee can" procedures. But even among the youngest children, a substantial minority also report saving at commercial institutions, although in many instances it is likely the parents do such saving for them. With age, we note a steady decline in home saving practices in favor of a corresponding rise in the incidence of commercial bank utilization.[28]

While no significant differences were found by sex or community of residence in the distribution of children selecting each mode of savings, an interesting difference by socioeconomic status emerged. Among middle-class children reporting saving, two-thirds said they used commercial or savings banks, compared to half of the working-class children. Working-class children, as we have seen above, are no less likely to report saving, but they do tend to do their saving at home (63 percent, N=155) more so than middle-class children (50 percent, N=59).[29]

With respect to how much money pupils save, the following observations are possible. First: 46 percent (55) of first graders and 24 percent (36) of third graders were unable to furnish our interviewers with even crude estimates as to the amount of their savings. This may indicate nothing more than children's tendencies to lose track of their pennies, nickels, and dimes as they accrue in a piggy bank. However, since many of these same children also report saving in a commercial institution, their lack of knowledge in this respect probably indicates something else, namely significant parental involvement in their savings activities. Among those children who did furnish such approximations to our interviewers, it was hardly surprising to find that savings start on a very modest level: the modal category among

TABLE 3.6
Percentage of children who report saving at
home and/or in commercial banks
by grade in school

	Grade in school*			
Child's saving practice:	1st	3rd	5th	7th
Save at home (piggy bank, etc.)	84.2% (101)	64.6% (104)	33.3% (18)	15.1% (8)
Saves at commercial bank or savings institution	32.5 (39)	52.8 (85)	72.2 (39)	96.2 (51)
Total cases:	120	161	54	53

* percentages may add to more than 100% since some children report both modes of saving.

first and third graders (24 percent, N=48) is less than five dollars saved. Since we have no way of checking the reliability of such estimates, there is little point in dwelling on such figures. Instead, these two observations—that parents are likely behind younger children's savings efforts and that the sums involved are typically quite small—are offered here in indirect support for the speculative proposition that the form of children's saving behavior may be more salient than the substance. That is to say, such findings may indicate that, in terms of children's growth and development, parents are more concerned with the mere fact that children exhibit evidence of developing the savings habit than they are with the extent of their children's savings.

Returning to our earlier question, it would be difficult to portray these children as acquisitive on the basis of their reports of savings

activities. May we then characterize them as inclined to defer gratification? To answer this, we can only point to the fact that two-thirds of
the first and third graders who reported saving money could specify
their savings goals to our interviewers. Among the most popular
items being saved for were toys and hobbies, spending money for
upcoming vacations, and presents for parents and siblings. A number
of first and third graders in this subsample (18 percent, $N=33$)
reported saving for such distant goals as the purchase one day of a car
or motorcycle, or for their college educations. While these last represent only a minority of cases, and our data on fifth and seventh
graders do not permit comparable assessments, we cannot dismiss
the possibility that the saving habits of a number of these children
are connected with the inclination to defer gratification, which has in
turn been considered indicative of commitment to the work ethic.[30]

Summary and Conclusions

Before attempting to draw conclusions on the basis of the evidence
just presented, it is important to acknowledge the limitations and
constraints operative in any investigation of the status of the work
ethic among children. To begin as simply as possible, work just does
not occupy the central position in the world of the child that it
supposedly does in the American culture in general. Very different
sets of expectations govern the work activities of children and adults.
For this reason, it would be unrealistic to employ adult standards to
evaluate children's commitment to the work ethic. Rather, we ought
to be looking, as it were, for the seeds of the work ethic, i.e., for
evidence of children's early predispositions toward the various attitudes, perceptions, and behaviors which indicate commitment to the
social institution of work.

Since children are not engaged in earning their livelihoods
through work, and since we have no first-hand access to the experiences of those children who do work or perform chores, we were
necessarily limited here to inferences based upon certain indirect
indicants of the work ethic. In this case, three such indicants were
considered: (1) children's regard for work, (2) their occupational
aspirations, and (3) their savings habits. Others might have been
added, but these at least offered the advantages of accessibility and
the relative simplicity required for testing children.

The outcome of our inquiries might best be described as a mixed lot.
On the one hand, we found evidence with respect to each of our
indicators that many children do indeed exhibit orientations which

suggest commitment to work. On the other hand, the levels of such commitment hardly seemed to justify an enthusiastic assertion that the Protestant ethic is thriving among the American middle- and working-class children sampled here. Nor did this level of commitment to the work ethic, except in occasional instances, seem to be predictably distributed according to such demographic variables as age, sex, community of residence, or socioeconomic status.

The above pattern applies about equally to our findings concerning each of the three indicators involved. While we found children overwhelmingly stating that they would work even if they did not need money,[31] further investigation suggested that their answers say more about their interest in money than in any intrinsic satisfaction they anticipated could be derived from working. This is not to suggest that interest in money could not be interpreted as positive evidence of commitment to the work ethic, merely that in the absence of more convincing evidence that such apparently acquisitive tendencies have their roots in a broader, more positive orientation toward work per se, we are reluctant to accept it as such.[32] We found, too, modest but growing positive regard for the challenge aspect of work, especially among the boys. Yet relatively few of our respondents could on this basis be objectively characterized as eager in their anticipation of occupational challenge. Children's regard for work, as measured by these children's responses to suggest the existence of any "anti-work" ethic among them. Yet their expressed attachment to work certainly falls considerably short of the ideal-typical version of the work ethic as it is usually portrayed.

With respect to children's aspirations, the findings are perhaps more positive. In keeping with the American Dream, the majority of children in the sample do project upward social mobility on the basis of comparisons between their stated occupational choices and reported parental occupations. Among boys, there is a clear age-related increase in the level of aspirations. Among girls, there is reason to think that initially high aspirations fade to some extent by the later years of elementary school. Ambition, however, is not espoused by all these children: The incidence of projected occupational inheritance among first and third grade boys is 36 percent (61), and 23 percent (101) of all children in the subsample actually project downward mobility.

We learned that most children save money in one fashion or another, that with age they are increasingly likely to deal with commercial banks or savings institutions for this purpose, and that their savings, while typically not amounting to much in absolute dollar value terms, are often earmarked for some future purpose. While our attempt to ascertain whether such findings suggest mere acquisitiveness of the inclination to defer gratification was admittedly speculative in nature, we are inclined to opt for the latter. If this speculation is correct, we may interpret these findings as positive evidence of a child-like commitment to the work ethic, one aspect of which involves frugal living with a view toward future contingencies.

What in general may we conclude on the basis of such findings? We can state with some assurance that certain seeds of the work ethic are in evidence among these children. We cannot, however, report that the Protestant ethic is in full bloom during the elementary years.

Assigning meaning to such results is more difficult, for it involves placing our findings in a broader context than our evidence strictly permits. Two very different interpretations of these findings are possible. Each follows in its own way from the same assumption, that what we have observed in children constitutes an incomplete or less-than-perfect version of the work ethic. Indeed, Weber was quite explicit in identifying the value orientations he termed the Protestant ethic as an "ideal type."[33] By implication, we would not expect absolute adherence to the abstract model among all or even most adult respondents, let alone among children.

The first interpretation views children's incomplete commitment to the work ethic as natural and predictable given their position in the life cycle. Earlier, with respect to children's work-related cognitions, we had no difficulty in accepting that while children evidence surprising amounts of knowledge, their work-related socialization was incomplete. Similarly, we have little reason to balk at the suggestion that such an interpretation be extended to children's internalization of the work ethic. Surely, it is plausible that what we have observed constitutes the early stages of developing commitment to the social institution of work. Certainly children's expressed willingness to work, growing preference for challenge, moderate aspirational levels, and their initiation (through savings habits) into the ranks of those who defer gratification could indicate that children have begun to move in the direction of commitment to the work ethic. We might even hypothesize that such fledgling behaviors serve to pave the way for a fullblown embracing of the work ethic and the American Dream during later adolescence or early adulthood. In short, we could, with little difficulty, accept children's apparently positive but incomplete commitments to work as "developmentally appropriate" for the elementary years. Indeed, we are inclined toward such an interpretation.

The alternative interpretation, however, cannot be dismissed. This involves the additional, and more cynical, assumption that the work ethic exists more as a managerial ideology than as a guiding principle taken into account by the millions. Sebastian DeGrazia has gone so far as to contend that "among workmen the work ethic never existed, and that if it gravely affected anyone it was the white-collar worker whose ears were more attuned to the preaching of the business classes."[34] If this is true—and we are by no means ready to concede as much—then we must entertain a very different possibility for the interpretation of our findings. We must admit the possibility that children's commitments to the Protestant ethic, incomplete though they may be, might in fact approximate adult orientations. In other words, children's growth may, in many instances, stop at about the level we have noted here. This is indeed an intriguing thesis, but tangential to our purposes and not strictly answerable given our present data. We would however offer two observations in this regard. First, if the "believers" in the work ethic tend to come disproportionately from the white-collar classes, as DeGrazia suggests, we would expect relatively clearcut differences by socioeconomic status in children's work orientations. Yet we have found little evidence of this. On the other hand, if commitment to work were as low as DeGrazia has contended, then we would expect to find children, as well as others, justifying work on grounds of its economic rewards rather than any intrinsic work-related satisfactions. Since this is exactly what we have found, we are in no position to reject such an interpretation.

In conclusion, we would like simply to reiterate our earlier statement that children do evidence some aspects of the Protestant ethic, but fall considerably short of the ideal-typical form of embracement of it. Whether our findings indicate the prevalence, as it were, of a "children's portion" of the work ethic or may be taken as evidence of the degree to which children's views approximate those of many adults depends upon the assumptions one is willing to make, and therefore remains an open question.

Notes

1.   Quoted in Studs Terkel, *Working* (New York: Avon Books, 1972), p. xi.
2.   The Special Task Force to the Secretary of Health, Education, and Welfare was commissioned on December 29, 1971, under the chairmanship of James O'Toole.
3.   *The Boston Globe,* for example, printed an extended series of articles dealing largely with dissatisfaction with work and the loss of commit-

ment to work on the part of Americans of all walks of life. See: Susan Trausch, "Work: Labor of Love or Lifetime of Drudgery?" Parts 1-7, *Boston Globe,* December 1-8, 1974. See also: Robert Lindsey, "Some Who Believe in a No-Work Ethic," *New York Times,* June 1, 1975.

4. Typically such concern has been more complex than mere conjecture as to the fate of the work ethic. Many have recognized that the persistence of values and attitudinal states is contingent upon many structural conditions, i.e., that the nature of work and the experiences associated with it influence work-related values and attitudes. Chinoy, for, example, documented how ambition is affected by the reality of the opportunity structure in the auto industry. See: Ely Chinoy, *Automobile Workers and the American Dream* (New York: Random House, 1955). More recently, Aronowitz eloquently described the frustration and resultant loss of job commitment of workers in General Motors' Lordstown auto assembly plant. See: Stanley Aronowitz, *False Promises: The Shaping of American Working Class Consciousness* (New York: McGraw-Hill, 1973), pp. 21-49. Sebastian DeGrazia, on the other hand, questions whether the work ethic had ever been strongly held by the working classes, contending that if it has ever been dominant it has only been among managerial or white collar workers. See: Sebastian DeGrazia, *Of Time, Work, and Leisure* (Garden City, N.Y.: Doubleday, 1964), p. 143.

5. For a review of such evidence, see: Special Task Force to the Secretary of Health, Education, and Welfare, *Work in America* (Cambridge, Mass.: M.I.T. Press, 1974), pp. 43-51.

6. Ivar Berg, " 'They Won't Work': The End of the Protestant Ethic and All That," in *Work and the Quality of Life: Resource Papers for Work in America,* ed. James O'Toole (Cambridge, Mass.: M.I.T. Press, 1974), pp. 27-38.

7. Max Weber, *The Protestant Ethic and the Spirit of Capitalism,* trans. Talcott Parsons (New York: Charles Scribner's Sons, 1958), pp. 47-94.

8. Robin M. Williams, Jr., *American Society* (New York: Alfred A. Knopf, 1957), chapter 11.

9. Moses Tischin, ed., *The American Gospel of Success* (Chicago: Quadrangle Books, 1965), p. 67.

10. The desire for extra money is reported by 40 percent of those in the first grade (N=18), and by 55 percent of those in the seventh (N=45). The "like to work" response is reported by 36 percent (N=16) of first grade respondents but by only 17 percent (N=14) of seventh graders. The proportion expressing a desire to keep occupied declines from 16 percent (N=7) to 8.5 percent (N=7) from grade one to grade seven respondents. Other reasons account for approximately 20 percent of responses in all grades. (X^2=23.72, p < .05).

11. Among boys 49 percent (88) who gave reasons said they would work in order to earn extra money. Among girls the comparable figure was 41 percent (79). With regard to the desire to be helpful, 15 percent (29) of the girls and 6 percent (11) of the boys specified this reason. (X^2=8.24, p < .05).

12. Leonard Goodwin, *Do the Poor Want to Work?* (Washington, D.C., 1972), p. 15.

13.   The items comprising our so-called "challenge" scale, it should be pointed out, also have a bearing on the closely related issue of the child's preference for autonomy in the work setting. The four items employed here were originally developed by L. K. Williams as part of an eight item inventory of "risk-taking propensity" for use in industrial settings. Here, our interest was restricted to those four items felt to be most directly indicative of positive orientation toward challenge and phrased in terms children could readily grasp.

Specifically, children received one point apiece for each of up to four responses indicating a positive orientation to challenge (asterisks identify these responses below). Children chose between paired alternative ways of completing the sentence "The kind of job I would like would be . . ." The paired choices were:

* a job where I am almost always on my own.
—— a job where there is nearly always someone around to help me on problems that I don't know how to handle.
* a job where I have to make many decisions myself.
—— a job where I have to make a few decisions by myself.
—— a job where I am almost always certain to do well.
* a job where I am usually pressed to the limit of my abilities.
* a job where I have the final say on my work.
—— a job where there is nearly always a person who will catch my mistakes.

See: L. K. Williams, "Measurement of Risk-Taking Propensity in Industrial Settings," (unpublished Ph.D., dissertation, University of Michigan, 1960). For a broader, more philosophical discussion of the significance of such phenomena as preference for challenge and autonomy in the broader context of human motivation, see: John Rawls, *A Theory of Justice* (Cambridge, Mass.: Harvard University Press, 1971) esp. pp. 424-433.

14.   Only 1.7 percent (9) of the children, it should be pointed out, scored the maximum of four points on this challenge index.

15.   Eleanor E. Maccoby, "Class Differences in Boys' Choices of Authority Roles," *Sociometry* 25 (March 1972), pp. 117-119.

16.   Admittedly our argument here is predicated upon the assumption that many American adults feel that poor people stay on welfare because they do not want to work. Goodwin ultimately concluded that the work orientations of the poor do not differ so greatly from those of the rest of the population, except that their commitment to work tends to deteriorate as a result of negative feedback in the form of frustrating and unpleasant work experiences. In support of our assumption here, note that Goodwin had found "outer city" (employed) black and white fathers less accepting of welfare than the unemployed black and white fathers in his sample. (p. 73) He also found that with respect to acceptability of welfare "that welfare mothers are transmitting to their sons a greater tolerance of government support than is found among white outer city families." (p. 67) Thus, while our assumption about the views of welfare of many Americans remain unproven, there is at least some

supporting evidence. See: Leonard Goodwin, *Do the Poor Want to Work?* (Washington, D.C.: the Brookings Institution, 1972).

17. Studs Terkel, *Hard Times* (New York: Avon Books, 1970), pp. 19-20. For a remarkably similar but expanded observation on the Great Depression and its impact upon personal identity, see: Lawrence Chenowith, *The American Dream of Success* (North Scituate, Mass.: Duxbury Press, 1974), pp. 63-89.

18. See, for example: Harry J. Parker, "29,000 Seventh Graders Have Made Occupational Choices," *Vocational Guidance Quarterly,* 11, (Autumn 1962), pp. 54-55.

19. Eli Ginzberg et al., *Occupational Choice* (New York: Columbia University Press, 1951).

20. Donald E. Super, "Consistency and Wisdom of Vocational Maturity in Ninth Grade," *Journal of Educational Psychology* 52 (February 1961), pp. 35-43.

21. Here we are following Turner who, in his 1964 study of California high school students, defined an ambitious student as one having "mobility orientations." See: Ralph Turner, *The Social Context of Ambition* (San Francisco: Chandler Publishing Co., 1964).

22. Wallace E. Lambert and Otto Klineberg, "Cultural Comparison of Boys' Occupational Aspirations," *British Journal of Social and Clinical Psychology* 3 (February 1963), pp. 56-65.

23. The sociological significance of the concept of the self-fulfilling prophecy was first recognized by W. I. Thomas, who observed that, "If men define situations as real they are real in their consequences," See: William I. Thomas and Dorothy Swaine Thomas, *The Child in America* (New York: Knopf, 1928), p. 572. The importance of the self-fulfilling prophecy in the occupational socialization of females has been underscored by Horner, who has suggested that women in competitive achievement situations are caught in a double bind because they have been socialized not only to fear failure, but to fear success as well. See: Mattina S. Horner, "Achievement-Related Conflicts in Women," *Journal of Social Issues* 38, no. 2 (1972), pp. 157-175.

24. The concept of "occupational inheritance" is variously interpreted in the sociological literature. A "strict" interpretation would employ the term only in references to cases in which the child enters the specific occupation of the parent, for example, in the case of going to work in the family business, or following one's parent into the profession of medicine. Here, we are using the term in a much broader sense in references to instances in which a child's stated occupational choice falls.

25. Max Weber, *The Protestant Ethic and the Spirit of Capitalism,* trans. Talcott Parsons (New York: Charles Scribner's Sons, 1958), pp. 17-27.

26. Ibid., p. 172.

27. For an excellent discussion of children's development of monetary concepts, see: Karl Schuessler and Anselm L. Strauss, "A Study of Concept Learning by Scale Analysis," *American Sociological Review* 15 (December 1950), pp. 752-762. See also: Anselm L. Straus, "The Development and Transformation of Monetary Meanings in the Child," *American Sociological Review* 17 (June 1952), pp. 275-286.

28. Some school systems enter into arrangements with local banks for

purposes of initiating savings habits among pupils by opening savings accounts for children and collecting their deposits weekly in the class-room. This was apparently not the case among participating schools in this study, as only one child reported having "school savings account."

29.   Percentages add to more than 100 percent because children report both modes of savings. There is little difference, however, by SES in the proportions of children who report both: 16 percent (19) of middle class children and 14 percent (35) of working class children report both.

30.   Ivar Berg, " 'They Won't Work,' " pp. 27-38.

31.   Tausky had asked blue-collar workers essentially the same question, which he considered an indicant of what he called *instrumentalism,* presumably a need to be active and productive. This is very much in keeping with our use of the question here. His question was phrased as follows: "If by some chance you had enough money to live comfortably without working, do you think that you would work anyway, or would you not work?" Among the blue-collar workers in his sample, 82 per-cent said yes. This compares quite favorably with our own findings of 76 percent ($N=391$) affirmative responses among elementary school chil-dren. He did not, however, continue to the next logical question of *why* people said yes, as we did. Since our respondents largely said yes for reasons of earning money above and beyond their needs, we cannot fully support the conclusion that affirmative answers necessarily indi-cate instrumentalism. See: Curt Tausky, "Meanings of Work Among Blue-Collar Men," paper presented at the meetings of the American Sociological Society, August, 1968, cited by John P. Robinson et al., eds., *Measures of Occupational Characteristics* (Ann Arbor, Mich.: Institute for Social Research, University of Michigan, 1969), pp. 221-222.

32.   This problem was familiar to Weber, who insisted that acquisitive behavior was neither new nor the principal point of his interest, except insofar as it derived from the positive evaluation of work as "calling" and accordingly had a sort of religious legitimation not previously found:

> A state of mind such as that expressed in the passages we have quoted from Franklin, and which called forth the applause of a whole people would both in ancient times and in the Middle Ages have been proscribed as the lowest form of avarice and as entirely lacking in self-respect . . . This is not wholly because the instinct of acquisition was in those times unknown or undeveloped, as has often been said. Nor because the . . . greed for gold was then or now less powerful outside bourgeois capitalism . . . as modern romanticists we are wont to believe. The difference between the capitalistic and pre-capitalistic spirits is not to be found at this point . . . Those who submitted to it [the impulse to make money] without reserve as an uncontrolled impulse . . . were by no means representatives of that attitude of mind from which the specific-ally modern capitalistic spirit is derived, and that is what matters.

See: Max Weber, *Protestant Ethic,* p. 56-57.
33.   Max Weber, *Protestant Ethic,* p. 71.
34.   Sebastian DeGrazia, *Of Time, Work and Leisure,* p. 143.

Chapter 4

Affective Work Orientations
and Sex-Typing

A *Boston Globe* reporter set out to learn the impact of work upon people in the 1970's. "I love my job. I'm a fee noter and I think it's great," responded one female interviewee. "I'd like to chuck it all and go drive a truck for a year," a psychiatrist confessed in candor, adding, "I've seen work do devastating things to human beings, turn them into addicts, into alcoholics." An $18,500-a-year computer programmer said, "I feel as though time is at my back with a stick . . . I'm trapped."[1]

Our observations to this point about children's work orientations have been restricted to matters of cognition and evaluation. But as the above quotes make clear, work also summons up feelings in people. To love one's work, to fear that it threatens to destroy one's identity, to experience frustration—all these are among a wide range of emotional reactions which work evokes in the individual. Historically, work has been defined thematically as both "curse" and "blessing."[2] Upon closer examination it should be clear that either of these social definitions necessarily implies certain affective states as well. If work seems as a curse visited upon the human race, is this not because it produces pain in so many? If work is perceived as a blessing, what is this except another way of saying it engenders feelings of happiness or fulfillment or dignity? Surely no analysis of work orientations would be complete without references to work-related feelings.

Feelings are inextricably linked to perceptions and beliefs, both as responses to such stimuli and as influences upon future cognitions. There is also a strong connection between affective states and attitudes; some would even equate the two.[3] It is clear that these phenomena cannot be readily dissociated from one another. In this chapter, we shall necessarily deal with each of these, but the emphasis is explicitly intended to be upon the affective. We shall inquire into children's "likes" and "dislikes" with respect to work. We shall seek the affective connotations involved in selected work-related perceptions. And we shall explore the rather complex phenomenon of stereotyping behavior, with an eye toward establishing the nature and extent of children's feelings with regard to work.

Children's Work-Related "Likes" and "Dislikes"

Feelings derive from experience.[4] Most children experience work less intensively than do most adults. Also, much of children's acquaintance with work comes second-hand, reaching them through adults, either in the form of direct transmission of occupational information or feelings, or by means of what children observe or surmise of adult work orientations. We must be wary, therefore, in our explorations of children's work-related feelings on at least two accounts. First, we ought not to expect children to exhibit the full range and depth of feelings which we might anticipate among adult respondents. Accordingly, we must be prepared to accept indirect measures of children's feelings, and to "read into" certain responses in the attempt to discern affective states. Second, we must proceed in the knowledge that much of what we are likely to find with respect to children's feelings about work may in fact be "inherited" directly from parents or others of significance. It would indeed be fascinating to trace the connections between, say, parental feelings and those of children in order to learn the relative proportions of "transmitted" feelings versus those, if any, which arise *de novo*. But we must be clear that we are in no position to assess such matters here.

We begin our investigation of children's feelings about work, perhaps ironically, with an assumption about the ways they relate to play. Few people would argue with the observation that children like play. In our culture, unlike certain others, the distinction between work and play is incisive, almost polar.[5] This suits our present purposes particularly well, for it places at our disposal a very simple method of surmising children's feelings about work. We need only ask children to compare work with play, a concept presumably associated with strong positive affective connotations, then note (1) whether children portray the two as antithetical,[6] and (2) the affective connotations implicit in their thematic responses.

We asked children whether in their opinions work and play were alike.[7] Our subjects obviously had no difficulty in formulating opinions on the matter: the percentage of "Don't know" responses was negligible (1 percent, N=5). Moreover, most children see little similarity between work and play. This is especially true in grades one, three, and five. We had wondered, in view of the fact that so much of children's time is consumed by play and so much of adults' is given over to work, whether children perhaps viewed work as the "adult version" of play. It is obvious that most of them do not, that the differences between the two activities are more salient than the points of comparison. However, this tendency seems less prominent among seventh graders. About a third of them either responded positively in terms of seeing such similarities or answered conditionally, i.e., that work and play *may* prove alike under certain sets of stated circumstances. No relationship was found between childrens responses in this regard and the variables of sex, socioeconomic status, or community of residence.

Since we were interested not so much in children's social definitions of work and play as in the affective connotations associated with such perceptions, we sought further information in this regard from those children who had seen no similarity between the two activities. Doing so, of course, introduced an obvious bias: We were asking pupils why work failed to compare to play, which we had begun by assuming they like. It was not our intention to commit the fallacy of affirming the consequent, but to ascertain the proportion of these children who contrasted the two on the basis of matters which were (at least arguably) affective in nature. Table 4.1 portrays the general types of criteria employed by those children who offered reasons why they did not consider work and play alike (N=467). By "potentially affective criteria" (a term which we acknowledge using in the broadest possible sense here) we refer to responses based upon the imputed presence or absence of such emotion-solving traits as fun, pleasure, seriousness, constraint, pressure, strain, etc. The term "matter-of-fact criteria" is not in any way meant to imply that the above affective dimensions are not necessarily factual, for it is not the accuracy of such assessments which now concerns us, merely whether they suggest the existence of work-related feelings. Instead, that phrase here refers to instances in which children contrasted work and play on the basis of matters we considered less likely to carry emotional connotations. For example, many noted that work was purposeful or goal-directed, whereas play was not; others observed that people earned money or expended more energy at one but not the other, etc.

TABLE 4.1

**Types of criteria employed by children
contrasting work and play
by grade in school***

	Grade in school			
Criteria:	1st	3rd	5th	7th
"Potentially affective criteria"	90.4% (103)	91.7% (133)	84.1% (106)	90.2% (74)
"Matter-of-fact criteria"	9.6 (11)	8.3 (12)	15.9 (20)	9.8 (8)
Total cases:	114	145	126	82

$$(x^2 = 4.52 \qquad p=ns)$$

* Percentages are based upon the number of children providing codable reasons for contrasting work and play.

Table 4.1 makes clear that the greater portion of children at each grade who contrasted work and play (as most did) did so for reasons we regarded as at least potentially connoting their feelings with respect to work. If we break down our findings more specifically, the response most frequently given was, to borrow the words of one child, that "Play is fun—work isn't!" Altogether, 51 percent (235) of those furnishing their reasons assessed the situation along such clearly affective lines. The remainder of responses included here under "potentially affective criteria" had to do in general with the unpleasantness or constraints associated with work or with the fact that it is often involuntarily performed. "No [work is not like play,]" said one child, "because it's hard—you have to get up early every day!" Said another: "You could do what you want and leave when you want in play. Play is easy." "When you work, you can't fool around or you'll get fired," observed another. Finally, in the eyes of one child, "Work is dangerous!" While admittedly such responses demonstrably involve children's perceptions, we submit that they also connote an underlying negativism, a *feeling,* if you will, about work.

As we wished some insight into the extent of this apparent "negativism" and whether it derived from children's impressions of the adult world of work or was perhaps rooted in their personal experiences, we pursued two disparate lines of inquiry with respect to children's work-related "likes" and "dislikes". First we asked children whether in their opinions most people liked work. After that, we inquired about their own feelings about work and the chores they do.

TABLE 4.2
Children's answers to "Do people like work?"
by grade in school

	Grade in school			
Response:	1st	3rd	5th	7th
Don't know	2.1% (4)	2.9% (6)	2.4% (5)	3.8% (5)
Yes	40.9 (79)	22.9 (47)	17.6 (37)	29.8 (39)
Conditional response	25.9 (50)	46.8 (96)	63.8 (134)	21.4 (59)
No	31.1 (60)	27.3 (56)	16.2 (34)	45.0 (59)
Total cases:	193	205	210	162

$$(x^2 = 97.98 \qquad p < .001)$$

The former inquiry provided a lesson about the relative intensity of children's work-related feelings. While work had not fared particularly well *in comparison with play,* the concept did not in general elicit such strongly negative connotations when children were asked the broader question of whether they thought people liked work. As Table 4.2 indicated, the response pattern on this item was most interesting indeed. Note once again the paucity of "Don't know" answers. Note, too, that from grades one through five there is a clear pattern of diminishing certainty, an age-related trend in favor of conditional answers. At least two interpretations, neither of which precludes the other, are possible here. If one concentrates on cognitive factors, it is quite reasonable to view this pattern as one of increasing realism with age. It is, after all, true that most workers cannot be subsumed under a blanket classification as either liking or disliking work. Some love their work; some hate it. Much of this depends upon the personality of the individual, and of course upon the nature of the job. Moreover, one may like working, per se, but not be especially pleased with his particular niche. Or, one may enjoy only certain aspects of the job or derive satisfaction solely from job perquisites (pay, standard of living it affords, status, etc.) rather than from actual task performance. Only about one first grader in four qualified his or her answer with some such observation, whereas about half the third graders and nearly two-thirds of the fifth graders did so—a pattern which we would have little difficulty accepting as indicative of cognitive growth or maturity. Indeed, this is the interpretation upon which we would insist, were it not for a break in the pattern among seventh grade respondents. Among the latter, the modal response was that people dislike work; the number of children answering conditionally declined considerably, largely in favor of negative responses.[8] Thus, while we do not wish to understate the growth in cognitive awareness suggested by such findings, we are also inclined toward an additional interpretation. We say "additional" because it is clear that seventh graders ought not suddenly to know *less* than younger respondents, nor can we accept that they are less "mature" with regard to this item alone. Rather, we believe, affect is also involved in such responses. Younger children, as the table also shows, tend to view the matter in black and white terms: 72 percent (139) of first graders, for example, expressed clear-cut opinions that most people either do or do not like work. With age comes increasing awareness and the corresponding inclination toward qualifying such opinions. But age may also bring an increase in negative work-related feelings to the point that, as children approach adolescence when affective factors perhaps weigh more heavily, affect may overtake cognition or at least strongly influence children's perceptions in such matters. We stress the tentative and conjectural nature of our observations in this regard.

We found no differences by socioeconomic status or community of residence with respect to children's responses to this question. Sex differences,[9] however, were quite pronounced in this area, and again subject to at least two interpretations. If one chooses to pursue the cognitive sort of explanation, girls might be termed more "mature" than boys by virtue of the fact that 49 percent (167) of the girls versus only 26.5 percent (106) of the boys answered in the more realistic, conditional sense. In terms of affect, it is equally possible to contend that boys are more strongly opinionated than girls in this matter, and hence arguably more affectively involved. In any event, it was clear that boys were significantly more negative (in either their work-related feelings or perceptions) than were girls, as 41 percent (163) of the boys expressed the opinion that people do *not* like work, compared to 24 percent (81) of the girls.[10]

Both these interpretations—that the results may be viewed as signs of cognitive development and/or as indicative of affective orientations toward work—are indeed plausible. Ultimately the issue reduces to whether one prefers to view children's "opinions" on the matter of whether people like to work as *perceptions,* in which case their accuracy is at issue, or as *projections* of children's own work-related feelings. Certainly a case could be made for either point of view; the two are not necessarily mutually exclusive.

While this confusion as to the relative importance of affect versus cognition cannot be resolved here, things do come into better focus when we turn our attention to purely subjective assessments. When we asked children about their feelings regarding their own work, nearly four in five at each grade level said they liked working, whether "child-work" in the true sense or merely the performance of routine household chores.[11] Whichever their earlier responses referred to—perceptions or feelings—it is apparent that many of these children adhere to a double standard of sorts. That is, many regard work as something which people in general dislike, yet they themselves have positive feelings with respect to at least the sorts of work typically performed by children. Further analysis revealed only two aspects of work which could be called "common" among children's responses as to *what* they liked about work: 27.5 percent (159) specified that they liked getting paid most of all, while an almost identical number (28 percent, N=160) singled out what we call "specific task pleasure." The latter term refers to some named aspect of a particular job or chore which the child said gave him/her pleasure. For example, children who did babysitting often specified that they enjoyed working with children. Others, especially boys, said that what they liked about yardwork was being out of doors or getting healthful exercise. One first grade girl allowed that she really looked forward to helping her mother wax the furniture because "you get to use a spray can."

When we asked children whether there were aspects of their work which they disliked, 17 percent (97) cited what we termed "task displeasure," often the very same aspects liked by different children. Some children, for example, did not like babysitting precisely because it involved the contact with younger children which others enjoyed. Others detested working in the garden because one gets filthy, which was a big attraction to some, etc. Another 11 percent (64) said they disliked work which was physically taxing. Most significantly, however, 42 percent (245) said that there was *nothing* about their childwork or chores which they disliked, a most convincing finding with respect to the potentially positive nature of work-related feelings.

We conclude this section with a few observations intended to place the above findings into sociological perspective. While we have had difficulty in assessing whether certain results had more to do with affect or cognition, perhaps it does not matter. The significance of these findings, we believe, lies in the fact that a fundamental dichotomy emerges in children's affective work orientations. On the one hand, as we have seen, many children ascribe to the general population either outright negative feelings about work or, as is increasingly the case with age, the potential for such negativism insofar as the expression of conditional answers amounts to the acknowledgment that people *may* dislike work. On the other hand, when it comes to their feelings about their own childwork or chores, children are overwhelmingly positive. The contrast in these two positions gives rise to two questions: (1) What does it all mean? and (2) Do we need to be concerned about the matter?

The meaning of these results is, frankly, unclear. They may indicate nothing more than the reification of common sense in the notion that childwork is, after all, relatively undemanding and inherently pleasant, consequently, perhaps easier to derive satisfaction from. Adult work is unfortunately often structured quite differently, and it does not guarantee satisfaction. Our findings may merely indicate that children know this as well as the rest of us do, in which case we need not be overly concerned about this dichotomy unless it is our intent to ameliorate the situation in general—a noble but unrealistic goal.

There is another way of viewing these findings, however, which would suggest we become concerned. We must keep in mind that while it is at times convenient to talk of the "culture of childhood," the dichotomy with which we are faced here is not simply a case of the disparity between two cultures; that of children who, by and large, like work versus that of adults, many of whom do not. The simple truth is that these children will ultimately enter the adult world, and they know it. Thus, an equally valid intepretation of these findings involves the view that children, while they might like work now, know, based upon their perceptions of adult work-related feelings, that the odds of their continuing to like it will decline. Sociologically, we might express our concern in terms of two somewhat similar concepts: anticipatory socialization and/or the self-fulling prophecy.

Merton coined the term "anticipatory socialization" in reference to the process by which people "take on the values of the non-membership group to which they aspire, find readier acceptance by that group, and make an easier adjustment to it."[12] If we consider adult workers as the group to which children aspire, we must be alert to the possibility that children's perceptions of adults as feeling negatively toward work might in turn lead to the eventual adjustment of their own (previously positive) feelings. To the extent therefore that children perceive such negativism as widespread, there is the possibility of the self-fulfilling prophecy.[13] In other words, children may attach normative significance to their observation and think they are in some sense "supposed to" dislike work, that such negative feelings are indeed signs of growing up. Such tendencies, if they do indeed exist, have their roots in matters of cognition. Thus, anyone concerned about such matters would do well to attend to the manner in which occupational feelings are presented to children. Particularly important in this regard is the role of the parent in defining the situation for the child. As Hartley has shown, young children typically view parents of both sexes as uncomfortable, indeed unhappy, about leaving their children to go off to their daily work.[14] It is doubtful that such perceptions arise from a vacuum. Certainly in many instances parents do in fact harbor negative feelings about their work, which children may surmise even if not directly told. On the other hand, one can also readily imagine a "trap" of sorts in which even parents who feel very positively about their work feign other sorts of responses so that their younger, relatively egocentric children will not feel they are alone in experiencing separation anxiety or that parents actually enjoy the activity which calls them away all day. Thus there is the potential in parent-child interaction not only for the accurate transmission to children of negative affect on the part of parents who do not in fact enjoy work, but also for the unfounded and therefore unnecessary transmission of such negative feelings even by parents who in reality feel quite positive about their work. Children's suggestibility in such matters should not be underestimated.

Occupational Sex-Typing in Childhood

Gender has traditionally played a most important part in the allocation of work roles and the division of labor in general. In recent times the ranks of those who question the arbitrariness of this practice have swelled, and dissent has become more vocal. As a result, sex-typed role assignments are no longer taken as "natural" in some quarters. Differential treatment according to sex has come to be regarded in many circles as a form of discrimination.

The concept of discrimination or prejudice is sociologically a most interesting one. In essence, it refers simply to differential treatment based upon ascriptive rather than achieved traits. Beneath such behavioral patterns, however, prejudice is rooted in both perceptions and feelings. Our task in the pages which follow will be to explore the early manifestations of children's affective orientations regarding the relationship between work and sex roles.

We must begin to clarify our terms, lest they create unnecessary confusion. "Stereotypes" are familiar to us in a variety of settings including the world of work. While the most commonly employed stereotypes, at least those to which we have become most sensitive, are racial or ethnic in nature, it is also widely recognized that people are very often "sex-typed" as well. But what does this ultimately mean? When we say that someone holds a stereotype, do we mean he/she *knows* something, or at least acts as if it were true? Or do we mean that person *feels* something? Indeed, can we even entertain the thought that stereotyping is a purely cognitive or purely affective process at all, or must we view it as a hybrid of sorts? Allport, in what remains the definitive theoretical work on the nature of prejudice, considered the phenomenon in relation to the psychological process of categorization. "A stereotype," he wrote, "is an exaggerated belief associated with a category. It's function is to justify (rationalize) our conduct in relation to that category . . . A stereotype is not identical with a category; it is a fixed idea which accompanies a category."

The usual *consequence* of a stereotype is that the category of person to which it refers—be it racial, ethnic, sexual or whatever—can no longer be held in mind as a "neutral, factual nonevaluative concept."[15] Thus to Allport, at least, it was clear: A stereotype is a form of imagery and, as such, cognitive in nature; affective and/or evaluative positions are not part of the stereotype, but follow from it.

Brown agreed in principle, noting that a stereotype differs from a social role in that it is purely cognitive, not normative. As he put it, "in the social stereotype we have categorical expectancies without prescriptions." He noted, too, that the problematic nature of stereotypes derives from a matter of controversy as to whether or not the category performs in such a way as to confirm the expectancy."[16]

That stereotyping must be considered a cognitive process does not, however, mean that it cannot also prove a most useful concept in our inquiry into children's work-related feelings. On the contrary, while the two may not be equated, it is clear that where stereotyping is known to exist, affect may often be expected to follow. There are at least two valid reasons for this expectation, especially as it pertains to our consideration of sex-typing. The first involves the critical issue of personal identity. Perhaps foremost among the various identities in our "kits" is the gender identity or sex role. We need not immerse ourselves in psychoanalytic theory to recognize that questions of identity elicit the deepest sort of emotional response. Moreover, normative factors are involved, too, in the form of differential expectations associated with each sex role. Havighurst, for example, made much of the importance of the child's learning the "appropriate" sex roles.[17] Thus, to the extent that stereotyping is functional for the individual, as Allport insisted it is, then the most likely outcome of sex-typing is reaffirmation or preservation of sexual identity. We fully expect affect to follow directly in many instances.

The second reason for the expectation that affect will be associated with stereotypes is perhaps best illustrated in the old story which used to be so popular among the advocates of the civil rights and women's liberation movements, both of which took as their principal objectives the combatting of stereotypes. It seems, or so the story would have it, that a white male had been the victim of an accident. Try as they might, the hospital emergency team could not stave off the inevitable. The patient's heart stopped. For all intents and purposes, he had died. Minutes later, as they were wheeling his body from the operating rom, he suddenly sat up and announced that he had come back from the dead, that he had been to heaven and had seen God. Amazed at this news and anxious to hear the first-hand account of the only living human to have had such an experience, those in the room pressed the man for details about what God was really like. "First of all," the man sighed, "she's black."

The story is of course apocryphal, but not without value in terms of the point to be made. Often the violation of a stereotype elicits a particular kind of affective response not ordinarily readily observable in non-problematic instances in which the evidence does not breach the imagery. Consider, if you will, the likely reactions of both the racists and the male chauvinists in the story upon hearing the patient's report. One possibility of course is a simple cognitive reaction: belief or disbelief. Either would likely be accompanied, we submit, by feelings ranging from surprise to annoyance, from apprehensiveness to an acute sense of fear. A more exaggerated but also extremely common response would be the experience of "cognitive dissonance" and the resultant need to reconcile the apparently authentic account of the witness with whatever previous image of God one might have a psychological need to preserve.[18] In such instances, affective responses have been considered by Festinger, et al., as integrally involved in this process of reconciliation: "Dissonance produces a discomfort and, correspondingly, there will arise pressures to reduce or eliminate the dissonance."[19]

Thus, while stereotyping cannot in itself be considered a matter of affect, there is certainly ample support for the assumption, which we shall be making here, that stereotypical imagery and feelings are often closely related. In this section we shall inquire into children's work-related feelings as they pertain to gender, and we shall be alert for such related matters as sex-typing and attitudes of traditionalism with regard to sex role preference. While the ensuing discussion will often deal with matters of cognition, it is also intended as the basis for inferences about children's feelings.

We begin our consideration of these issues with a simple but important question: Do occupations arouse generally positive or negative feelings in children? To answer this, we utilized the Primary Occupational Feelings Inventory, developed by House and her colleagues for the purpose of ascertaining the relative levels of positive and negative affect produced in children by selected occupational imagery.[20] Briefly, the instrument involves the presentation of visual stimuli in the form of pictures of objects readily identifiable with certain occupations (example: stethescope as symbol for physician). Once children's attention has been directed to the pictorial cue before them, they are informed of the name of the occupation in question.[21] Then they are asked to record their subjective reactions to it ("How would you feel if you were a ——?") by checking one of three response boxes: smiling face (positive), frowning face (negative), empty box (neutral or unknown feelings, non-recognition of occupation).

Our findings in general confirm Tyler's observation that positive affective responses outweigh negative and indifferent responses during the early elementary years.[22] When the instrument was administered to first graders in our sample (N=203) the mean proportion of positive answers for the twenty occupations involved (59 percent) was more than twice that of negative responses (27.5 percent). The mean proportion of "Don't know" and/or neutral responses was 16.5 percent. In only two cases of rather low status jobs (custodian and garbage collector) did the incidence of "frowns" surpass that of "smiles." Thus, as a baseline against which other findings below may be judged, we note a general pattern of positive feelings or approbation.

TABLE 4.3
Positive affective responses (percentage of "smiles")
by typically male occupations
by sex

Occupation:	Boys	Girls	
Mechanic	69.8%	25.0%	**
Mail carrier	64.7	41.0	*
Factory worker	52.5	26.5	**
Taxi driver	58.8	39.8	*
Police officer	89.8	61.9	**
Construction worker	73.7	28.6	**
Gas station attendant	68.6	39.8	**
Garbage collector	49.2	26.5	*
Custodian	31.7	29.8	
Doctor	61.3	48.8	
Pilot	73.1	60.7	
Dentist	62.0	64.6	
Bus driver	63.9	57.1	
Means:	63.0%	42.3%	
Total cases:	119	84	

* = chi-square significant at .01 level
**= chi-square significant at .001 level

Turning to the issue of gender, we note pronounced differences in predictable directions when children's responses to these items were controlled by the child's sex. For purposes of display, the occupations are divided here along traditional lines with regard to the gender of the usual role occupant. Table 4.3 for example, shows a mean positive response rate of 63 percent among the boys versus 42 percent among the girls with respect to the thirteen typically male occupations presented in the inventory. Table 4.4 shows the reverse to be true, but more strongly, with respect to the five occupations ordinarily occupied by females: 77.5 percent of girls versus only 38 percent of the boys indicated the "smiles" in these instances. With respect to the individual items, the majority of the typically male occupations were rated significantly more positively by the boys. Among the girls, each of the five typically female occupations received significantly higher scores. In the case of two occupations (included for purposes of control) which cannot be readily sex-typed (movie star and grocery clerk) it is of interest that the observed differences in both cases did not prove statistically significant.

TABLE 4.4
Positive affective responses (percentage of "smiles")
by typically female occupations
by sex

Occupation:	Boys	Girls	
Nurse	23.5%	78.6%	**
Secretary	36.4	79.9	**
Teacher	51.7	85.5	**
Librarian	45.4	83.1	**
Hairdresser	31.7	60.2	**
Means:	37.8%	77.5%	
Total cases:	119	84	

**= chi-square significant at .001 level

Such findings are meaningful in several respects. In the first place, they corroborate the previous findings of Looft that sex-typing plays an important role in the work orientations of young girls.[23] Beyond that, they provide us with a basis for comparing the sexes in this regard. In so doing, we find indirect support for Hartley's contention that the pressures experienced by young boys to conform to prescribed sex roles are more acute than those faced by girls.[24] At least, we infer this to be the the case on the basis of differences in the relative proportions of boys and girls expressing positive feelings about occupations ordinarily predominantly occupied by members of the opposite sex. To be sure, young children of both sexes seem rigid in their sex-specific feelings, but if we concentrate on such "crossover approbation" it would seem that the boys are more negativistic and inflexible than the girls. If we compare, for example, the ratios of boys and girls respectively who expressed positive feelings in relation to the "opposite sex" occupations listed, we find that boys are less than half as likely (1 to 2.05) to have such feelings about female occupations as girls. On the other hand, the proportions of girls expressing positive feelings about male occupations was two-thirds (1 to 1.49) that of boys. We take boys' apparently lower inclinations to "crossover" as evidence in indirect support of Hartley's position that sex-specific role prescriptions are more acute in boys. Such findings would also appear to cast doubt on the validity of concern expressed regarding the "feminization" of young children through extensive contact with female teachers.[25]

Our next question concerned the strength of children's stereotyped notions with respect to occupations. To explore this matter, we presented children with five pictures as stimuli for oral or written discussion of the depicted occupations.[26] Keeping in mind our earlier observation about the tendency for affect to be revealed when stereotypes are violated, two of the drawings depict workers in situations which defy the "normal" sex-typed conceptions by positing women performers in typically male occupational roles. Actually, while this "violation"is clear in the first case (a female airline pilot), the person in the other (a physician examining a patient) is intentionally drawn in a way that one cannot be certain of the sex, i.e., the person has a slight build, is wearing pants and a lab-type coat, and has a short "uni-sex" Afro-style haircut. The other three pictures (male scientist, male farmer, female teacher) were presented as "controls," since they do not violate prevailing sex stereotypes.

The extent to which children expressed surprise, approval or disapproval, or even failed to perceive the "violations," we suggest, may serve as indicants of the degree of strength of their stereotypes. Results here are difficult to assess on a quantitative basis because one cannot be sure whether a child's failure to react means the absence of a stereotype, that the imagery is weak or unimportant, or merely that the child is not particularly verbal. On the other hand, as we shall see, there is little difficulty in assessing the qualitative meaning of the responses we did receive. The excerpts which follow are taken from research which was exploratory in nature and should be regarded as such. While they may *suggest* certain impressions, they can do no more.

We begin with children's responses to the picture of the female airline pilot. Among first and third graders interviewed, 21 percent (71) verbalized what our interviewers regarded as amusement or surprise at the prospect of a female pilot. Only 5 percent (18) of the fifth and seventh graders, however, put such expressions of surprise into writing. Below, we present selected responses chosen to convey a sense of children's reactions. They are organized very generally into categories according to how extreme the reaction appeared to be.

Our first category includes a very small minority of children, who are fully aware of the stereotype, but willing, even eager, to support its violation. "That's the first lady pilot," said a fifth grade girl, "She's trying to outsmart men. She's a women's libber'." Eleven year old Diane agreed, adding "Women's Lib women are equal to men. Girls are better than men. If men can fly, women can fly." A classmate, also female, called the depicted woman "courageous" for showing her skills. Not to be outdone, twelve-year-old Dick said, ". . . and if you want to know if there's anything wrong with a woman pilot, I say no." It is of interest to note that no such answers were given by first or third graders. In any case, children in this category were few and far between.

Our second group, and by far the majority, is comprised of children who evidence awareness of the stereotype, but no strong reaction to it. These are the students who merely mention sex in identifying the occupation and/or point out that it is unusual to find a woman airline pilot. While not all of these children's reactions could be character- ized as surprise, it was nonetheless plain that the idea of a female pilot was foreign to most of them. Altogether, two-thirds of all re- spondents (68 percent, N=470) specifically mentioned sex, referring to "a lady pilot," or "a lady flying a plane." This is interesting insofar as virtually *none* of the responses for the control picture of the scien- tist, for example, used the term a "man scientist." One is reminded of Dr. Johnson's alleged remark comparing a woman preacher to a talking dog. The wonder of it all, he noted, lay not in how well she performed, but that she performed in the role at all. "This pilot is a girl pilot, which is unusual," observed a first grade boy typical of this group.

Not all children were so restrained. "[It's] a lady pilot. It's crazy!" opined another first grade boy who was representative of the disap- provers. "Girls are not good pilots," said Angela, age six. James, her classmate went a step further, offering a theory: "[It's] an airline pilot. It's a girl! Who ever heard of that? It's dumb, cause they might forget how to fly. Women have smaller brains than men."

Some, especially the boys, were even less kind in appraising the prospect of a female pilot. Bruce, a fifth grade boy wrote: "She's flying an airplane. She looks like she's been through a mental hospital. She looks like a mental case. I'd like to do what she's doing, but she doesn't look the right type."

Others who disapproved offered reasons for their opinions that men are more capable than women of being pilots. "Men are usually pilots," observed nine-year-old Andy, "[because] they have more strength to control the plane in a storm." Eight-year-old Tommy would add to that, "Men usually fly planes because they're not afraid of heights."

Respondents in our next category did not so much express surprise or disapproval as merely insist upon strict conformity to traditionally prescribed sex roles for airline personnel. "[It's] a lady driving a plane. I can't believe it. Women are supposed to be stewardesses. Pilots are usually men." That was the way one first grade boy summed up the situation. Another boy, age seven, had to sort it out in the presence of the interviewer. "A pilot. A lady pilot. Never seen one. I think she is a stewardess. Ladies are always stewardesses." Often, it was apparent that a child thought "pilot" and "stewardess" were equivalent terms referring, respectively, to males and females who fly planes. "I think that women who drive planes are called stewardesses," said a first grade girl. It was difficult to tell whether seven-year-old Randy meant to be as cynical as he sounded when he made reference to a prominent airline's use of hostesses names in its advertising campaign. "[It's] Linda or Barbara. She's working on a jet. She's looking for a guy."

Our next class of respondents differed from the disapprovers only in degree. They might be called the "prophets of doom" based upon their assessments of women's abilities to fly. In a classic example of understated concern, six-year-old Ronald appraised the situation as follows: "It's funny, ladies crash a little." "It's a lady flying a plane . . . *Trying* to drive an airplane. They are going into a wall," warned Charles, a fifth grader. Nor were worries confined to the boys. Said seven-year-old Kathy: "It's a girl pilot. She drives airplanes and sometimes if she shifts wrong, the plane will turn over and fall in the river." Finally, there is Joe, a third grader:

> . . . Ladies don't know all the right stuff to do. Ladies aren't fit to be pilots. They might not learn right and they might make a mistake, and a lot of people could get killed. I could see them being truck drivers in *small* trucks, or being the manager of a building maybe, but not a pilot. They're not that strong.

Our final category of respondents to the pilot picture, while involving only a relatively few children, is perhaps the most interesting, for

it is comprised of cases in which children are likely trying to resolve
cognitive dissonance produced by the depicted violation of the stereotype. In a few instances, the child resolved the dissonance by a simple
denial. For example, one first grade boy while looking at the female
in the picture, told our interviewer, "He is driving an airplane."
Another replied simply, "A lady pilot. There is no such thing," and
thereby apparently resolved the need to reconcile the picture with the
stereotype he obviously held. A seventh grade boy recognized that the
woman was flying the plane, but could not accept the obvious implication that she was a pilot. He identified her as "a hijacker."

The responses to the pilot picture certainly convey a sense that
children have internalized sex-specific occupational categories. They
also suggest that many children feel sufficiently strongly about such
matters as to spontaneously express very emphatic opinions as to the
appropriateness of a woman's occupying the role. It should be noted
that at no time were children asked specifically for their feelings or
evaluations of the subject matter, merely for what they knew of
people in such occupations. Thus, the *unsolicited* emergence of so
many strong opinions would certainly give testimony to the strength
of occupational sex-typing during childhood.

The drawing of the physician in such a way that sex could not be
definitely determined on the basis of the features depicted was intended to explore a slightly different aspect of stereotyping. Here the
question was, given that stereotyping takes place, how binding is it?
How much does it limit perceptions? Do violations of stereotypes
present children with particular sorts of problems? In order to provide opportunity to assess such matters, it was decided not only to
minimize the depicted person's gender as an outright "clue," but also
to make it plain that the person was indeed a physician. Thus, the
doctor is drawn, stethescope in hand, in the act of examining a
patient. To further load the dice, at least for those children who could
read, a diploma which reads "Dr. A. Smith, Rutgers Medical School"
occupied a very prominent position in the background of the picture.
Children were then presented with the picture and asked to tell (or
write, as the case may be) what is the occupation of the person and
what they know of people who do that sort of work.

We have no estimate of the proportions of children who, had they
seen the depicted person in a different setting, would have identified
it as a male or female. Nor do we know how many of these children
have had experiences with female physicians of which, unlike female
pilots, there are a considerable number. Thus, the data which follow
cannot be regarded as accurate assessments of the proportions of

children falling into certain categories. They are included to convey on an impressionistic basis the ways in which stereotypes seem to influence children's perceptions.

Although we presume the stereotype of the physician usually refers to a male, the incidence of expressed surprise (1 percent, N=8) was negligible. While there is the temptation to interpret this as evidence that children either view the picture as male or are familiar with female physicians, this is not necessarily the case. In most cases, children either mentioned sex or used a sex-specific personal pronoun, often after considerable effort on the interviewer's part to prolong the conversation until they did so. (Interviewers were instructed not to bias answers by directly asking the gender of the depicted person, except in cases in which the child raised the question or acknowledged being confused on that account. In such instances, the interviewer merely turned the question back to the child by asking "Which do *you* think it is?") Among those cases in which the child's perception of gender were codable (N=509), 68 percent (348) ultimately identified the picture as that of a male, 29 percent (149) as female, and 3.5 percent (12) explicitly said they could not decide.

Many of first graders' reading levels were such as to render the diploma clue useless, thereby giving the child more latitude in deciding upon the occupation depicted. About half the first graders (51 percent, N=87) who mentioned gender saw this as a picture of a woman; 25 percent (43) also said it was a *nurse* rather than a doctor. These figures give us a crude estimate of the proportions of children who *might* otherwise have identified the picture in that way had the diploma not been there to force them to "think doctor," as it were. We take this as our "control" in a most elementary and imprecise sense.

The situation becomes especially interesting when one considers the possibilities available to the child in perceiving the picture. We know that among third, fifth, and seventh graders—who could read the diploma cue—the percentage of children seeing the picture as male rises to 78 percent (162) of those who specified gender, and the percentage of those seeing a doctor rises to 95 percent (332). Thus, if our previous control estimate has any value at all, we can conclude that many children who would otherwise have "seen" a female and/or a nurse instead, due to the inescapable diploma, not only see a doctor, but consequently a male as well.

The possibilities for cognitive dissonance are particularly intriguing in this instance, for there are not one but two possibilities for broken "sets" of imagery. Assuming that sex stereotypes prevail, many children may be presumed to bring two simple equations to the situation: (1) doctor = male; (2) nurse = female. Presumably, also, these equations are reversible, and thus *may* translate syllogistically into: (1) if male, then doctor; (2) if female, then nurse. Indeed, in support of the notion that sex-typing is quite strong among these children, we can offer numerous examples in which it is obvious that the child conceives of woman and doctor as mutually exclusive terms. And, we can offer classic examples of children's attempts to resolve cognitive dissonance in this regard.

A few representative excerpts should make clear the mutually exclusive natures of the categories in the eyes of many children. Teddy, age six, identified the picture as that of a nurse. "She's a girl," he said, "She has to be a nurse." Seven-year-old Bobby weathered some initial confusion quite readily: "[It's] a doctor. No—a nurse, 'cause it's a girl."

Eight-year-old Annie, while admitting to the possibility of a female doctor, reckoned it unlikely:

R: A doctor. She . . . He . . . has a patient.
I: Which do you mean, he or she?
R: He. It looks like a she, but it's a he.
I: How do you know?
R: The only way that I know is that it says "doctor." But I guess it *could* be a Doctor *Allan* Smith or Doctor *Anne* Smith.

This reconstructed interview with six-year-old Rodney illustrates the way in which the resolution of cognitive dissonance takes place:

R: A doctor? Is this a doctor or a nurse?
I: Which do you think it is?
R: It looks like a doctor. But it looks like a girl.
I: Can you tell me about it?
R: A doctor checks you up in case you have a cold or post nasal drip. A doctor has a special telescope called a fessascope [sic] and he checks your heart.
I: So you've decided it's a *he?* How could you tell?
R: Because of the shoes.

In such instances, the lengths to which children went to justify answers they knew *had* to be right suggest how readily children's perceptions follow from the stereotypes they bring to the situation. A look at the actual picture shows that only one shoe is visible, and it is drawn with virtually no detail. Yet, as we have seen, that was how one child allegedly *knew* this was a doctor. In support of our contention that such perceptions are subject to influence, we offer the response of six-year-old Theresa to the same picture: "It's a nurse, because she has fingernails, and girl's shoes on." The same shoe serves as evidence confirming a very different answer. Moreover, while men's fingernails may be kept shorter than those of many women, few would deny their existence. But no matter: A close look at the picture reveals that only one of the person's hands is visible, and it is clenched—not a fingernail in sight!

Finally, in illustration of the difficulty involved in resolving such dissonance, we offer a few classic and not entirely unrepresentative cases.

Jamie, age 9, appraised the situation in this way:

> This is another funny picture. I didn't know if it was a man, or a lady, or a man. Then I saw the sign. It must be a man, 'cause it's a doctor. And it must be a man 'cause it says "Dr. A. Smith." And there's only one girl's name with A, and that's Anne. And that wouldn't be a doctor's name.

In the pre-test, one child actually topped that. He knew it was a doctor "because it said 'Dr. A. Smith' and . . ." after a long, thoughtful pause he exclaimed that "Smith is a boy's name."

We rest our case.

Our final set of observations on the subject of sex-typing have to do with occupational imagery among first and third graders. Specifically, we wondered how traditional children's imagery would be with regard to sex roles. Given the findings already reported, it is not surprising that we found young children in general to be very traditionalistic in this aspect of their work orientations.

Here, the research strategy involved exploitation of young children's enjoyment of drawing. We presented first and third graders with a booklet comprised of three empty "frames." They were then told they would have ten minutes to draw and color a certain picture in each frame. We asked them to draw the first thing which came to mind when they heard the phrases "a man working," "a woman working," and "me working when I grow up," respectively. Since in many cases the contents of these drawings would not be evident to the observer, our interviewers circulated among children as they drew, recording "titles" for each picture. Thus, our data are not the pictures per se, but children's verbal accounts of what they were drawing in each of the three cases. Such descriptions were then coded according to whether the depicted activities were traditionally male, traditionally female, or not sex-typed.

Our findings suggest that sex-typing may be more pronounced with regard to male activities as portrayed in children's occupational imagery. The great majority of pupils (88 percent, N=303) drew the man performing activities traditionally allocated to males. Very often these activities involved obvious physical exertion: law enforcement, fire fighting, carpentry, construction, mechanics, athletics, heavy equipment operations, and military activities. While boys were slightly more inclined toward such drawings, the girls did not lag far behind.[27] While the tendency to sex-type female activities was also clearly present (71 percent, N=243), it was somewhat less pronounced. There were also sex differences with respect to the female picture: 18 percent (38) of the boys, for example, drew her in a traditionally male activity, versus only 9 percent (12) of the girls.[28] Cooking, housecleaning, nursing, teaching, and secretarial/clerical work were among the most popular activities.

When it came to their projections of their own occupational futures, children's drawings conformed almost exactly to the traditionalistic pattern established with respect to their imagery of other workers. That is to say, 86 percent (180) of the boys depicted themselves in traditional sex roles, as did 64 percent (86) of the girls. While about one girl in seven saw herself in a traditionally male role (such as doctor or scientist) the proportion of boys projecting themselves into female activities was negligible. The percentage of girls opting for activities not readily sex-typed (like general office work, entertainment, or operating a cash register) was twice that for boys (22 percent, N=30; to 12 percent, N=25).[29]

Obviously, children were consistent in their sex-typing. About half of them (52 percent, N=176) in fact were traditionalistic on *all three* drawings. Fully 86 percent (291) made at least two such selections in three. Boys (58 percent, N=119) were significantly more likely than girls (43.5 percent, N=57) to have done so on all three drawings.[30]

Summary

We set out in this chapter to explore two distinct, but often closely related, aspects of children's orientations: work-related feelings and the stereotyping of occupations by sex. In general, we found children to have a wide range of feelings with regard to work. Many, we learned, seem to adhere to a double standard. While they sense that work is in general disliked, they themselves are relatively positive in their feelings about it. There is some suggestion in the data, however, that children begin to fall victim to this negativism, as we have called it, by the later years of elementary school.

Children from the earliest grades at which we tested very definitely showed signs of occupational stereotyping on the basis of sex. We noted response patterns which suggest, for example, that children not only employ gender as a relevant category in their occupational thinking, but are also strongly influenced by the reification of such categorical thinking both in terms of their feelings and their future perceptions. While in some cases, our data were "soft" they nonetheless convey a sense of the strength of stereotypical thinking in children's work orientations.

Notes

1. These statements are excerpted from interviews presented in a series of articles dealing largely with worker dissatisfaction among Americans of all walks of life. See: Susan Trausch, "Work: Labor of Love or Lifetime of Drudgery," Parts 1-7, *Boston Globe*, December 1-8, 1974.

2. Adriano Tilgher, *Homo Faber: Work Through the Ages*, trans. Dorothy Canfield Fisher (Chicago: Henry Regnery Co., 1958).

3. For purposes of clarity we need to define a few crucial terms as they will be used here. *Cognition* refers to the process of knowing or perceiving in the broadest sense, without regard to the objectivity of what is "known." It thus includes social definitions of all sorts: perceptions, beliefs, even misconceptions. By *feelings,* we mean affective or emotional states of a clearly subjective nature, classifiable very generally as either positive or negative, and capable of variation in terms of the intensity with which they are experienced. *Attitudes,* for our purposes, refer to positive or negative evaluations of some social object which ordinarily rest upon or follow from both cognitive and affective states. There has long been disagreement within the ranks of social psychologists with respect to the relationship between attitudes, feelings, and cognitions. For example, many would draw no distinction between feelings and attitudes, etc. For a concise but excellent critical review of much of the extensive literature in regard, see: Robert A. Baron, Donn Byrne, and William Griffitt, *Social Psychology: Understanding Human Interaction* (Boston: Allyn and Bacon, 1974), pp. 35-36, pp. 164-169.

4. Donn Byrne and Gerald L. Clorr, "A Reinforcement Model of Evaluative Responses," *Personality: An International Journal* 1 (Summer 1970), pp. 103-128.

5. Anthropologists have pointed out that not all cultures differentiate so sharply as we do between work and play, nor do they all erect rigid age-related role prescriptions with regard to the appropriateness of same. Leighton and Kluckholn, for example, noted striking differences in this regard between the cultures of the Navaho of the American Southwest and the so-called Anglo or standard American culture:

It is a question of attached values, this difference between the white and the Navaho point of view. The Navaho expects to work . . . nor is play only for children and work only for adults; all ages do both as it becomes possible and necessary, as a natural and expected matter . . . The white child expects to play . . . There seems to be an overall difference in emphasis . . . between white and Navaho attitudes.

See: Dorothy Leighton and Clyde Kluckhohn, *Children of the People: The Navaho and His Development* (Cambridge, Mass.: Harvard University Press, 1947), pp. 169-170.

6. Smith and Proshansky in investigating the meanings of work and play among children and adolescents did find evidence that the concepts were antithetical, or at least mutually exclusive for many children. See: Robert Smith and Harold Proshansky, *Conceptions of Work, Plan, Competence and Occupation in Junior and Senior High School Students: Final Report* (Ann Arbor, Mich.: Institute for Social Research, University of Michigan, 1967), pp. 242-243.

7. First, third, and fifth graders answered the question as if it were posed by a hypothetical alien. Seventh graders were asked directly to compare work and play. Fifth and seventh graders responded to their respective questionnaires in writing; first and third graders were interviewed.

8. Seventh graders answered the question in a different format than did children in grades one, three and five. However, it would not appear that seventh graders' departure here from the pattern of answers is related to the way the question is asked. For one thing, the questions were phrased along quite similar lines. The younger children were asked: "Do most people like working?" Seventh graders were asked: "Do you think most people like or dislike working? Explain your answer fully." Nor do we believe that seventh graders elected not to explain conditional answers because of the need to write them. Fifth graders, it should be recalled, wrote their answers and two thirds of them answered conditionally.

9. The difference on the "yes" answer was 7 percentage points; on the "no" answer, 17 percentage points; and for conditional responses, 23 percentage points. $(X^2 = 10.43, p < .05)$.

10. In the previous chapter it was noted that children, especially boys, evidence at least modest commitment to the work ethic. Here, we are noting that many children, again especially boys, apparently feel that most people do not like work. One might wonder if such findings are inconsistent, perhaps even mutually exclusive of one another. We suggest that this is not necessarily the case. The essence of commitment to the work ethic lies in the conviction that work is *important,* ideally for religious or moral reasons. This question, theoretically at least, is separate from the matter of children's feelings, per se. That is to say, one does not necessarily have to *like* work to consider it important or endowed with moral significance.

11. Among first graders, 78 percent (150) respondents said they liked work. Among third, fifth and seventh graders, the comparable figures were 85

percent (175), 74 percent (156), and 75 percent (98). Obviously, the tendency to express positive feelings about one's own work was not significantly related to grade in school. Nor did it vary by sex, community of residence, or socioeconomic status.

12. Robert K. Merton, *Social Theory and Social Structure* (New York: Free Press, 1968), p. 319.

13. The concept of the self-fulfilling prophecy was first brought to the attention of sociologists by W. I. Thomas in his famous dictum, "If men define situations as real they are real in their consequences." See: William I. Thomas and Dorothea Swaine Thomas, *The Child in America* (New York: Knopf, 1928) p. 572.

14. Ruth E. Hartley, "Children's Concepts of Male and Female Roles," *Merrill-Palmer Quarterly* 6 (Summer-Fall 1960), pp. 83-91.

15. Gordon W. Allport, *The Nature of Prejudice* (Garden City, N.Y.: Anchor Books, 1958), p. 187.

16. Roger Brown, *Social Psychology* (New York: Free Press, 1965), p. 173.

17. Robert J. Havighurst, "Youth in Exploration and Man Emergent," in Henry Borow ed., *Man in a World at Work* (Cambridge, Mass.: Houghton-Mifflin, 1964), pp. 215-236.

18. So called "dissonance theory" has in recent years become an extremely influential force within social psychology. For a general explanation of the theory by its earliest and principal proponent, see: Leon A. Festinger, *A Theory of Cognitive Dissonance* (New York: Row, Peterson, 1957).

19. Leon Festinger, Henry W. Riecken, and Stanley Schachter, *When Prophecy Fails* (New York: Harper and Row, 1956), p. 26.

20. The primary Occupational Feelings Inventory was originally developed by Professor Elaine House of Rutgers University in association with Grace Bingham and Donna Cubit-Swayer as part of the efforts of the Commission on the Occupational Status of Women, Eastern Region, National Vocational Guidance Association.

21. For a complete list of the symbols and the occupations with which they are associated, see the Primary Occupational Feelings Inventory. Also, it bears mentioning that no gender was mentioned in the presentation of occupational titles to children. Thus, for example, police officer was used instead of policeman etc.

22. Leona E. Tyler, "The Development of Vocational Interests I: The Organization of Likes and Dislikes in Ten-Year-Old Children," *Journal of Genetic Psychology* 86 (March 1955), pp. 34-44.

23. William R. Looft, "Vocational Aspirations of Second Grade Girls," *Psychological Reports,* 28 (February 1971), pp. 241-242.

24. Ruth E. Hartley, "Sex Role Pressures and the Socialization of the Male Child," *Psychological Reports* 5 (September 1959), pp. 457-468.

25. Biber et al. have investigated teachers' "instructional contact" with pre-school children. While they did note that teachers typically have more contact with girls in the classroom, they found little to suggest that teachers reward "female behavior," per se, more than they do "male behavior." See: Henry Biber, Louise B. Miller, and Jean L. Dyer, "Feminization in Preschool," *Developmental Psychology* 7 (July 1972), p. 86. See also: Louise B. Miller, Jean L. Dyer, and Henry Biber,

Experimental Variables of Head Start Curricula: A Comparison of Current Approaches: Annual Progress Report (Louisville, Ky.: University of Louisville, 1970).

26. Children in grades one and three were typically interviewed, allowing opportunity for probe questions. Children in grades five and seven were gathered into small groups and presented with the pictures and asked to write of their knowledge and impressions of the occupations. With respect to the use of pictures as stimuli, we are following in many respects a procedure employed by Schlossberg and Goodman. See: Nancy K. Schlossberg and June Goodman, "A Woman's Place: Children's Sex Stereotyping of Occupations," *Vocational Guidance Quarterly,* 20 (June 1972), pp. 266-270.

27. Specifically, 91 percent (191) of first and third grade boys' and 82 percent of the girls' pictures of men working were sex-typed ($X^2=9.04$, $p < .05$).

28. $X^2=10.08$, $p < .01$.

29. $X^2=197.97$, $p < .001$.

30. $X^2=9.49$, $p < .05$.

Chapter 5

Children's Awareness of Social Class

Q: Are some people more important than others?
A: No, all are the same, except some.

Marcie, age 10

"All animals are created equal. But some animals are more equal than others."[1] In those words uttered by one of the fictional citizens of the *Animal Farm*, George Orwell satirized an important aspect of the human condition as he saw it. However attractive or useful our egalitarian myths may be, the social order as we have known it is structured along very different lines. Even for those who would deny it or wish it away, social stratification[2] has been an imposing fact of life. In this chapter, we take up the question of children's awareness of the "pecking order," if you will, in our society. Since social class is so closely related to occupational matters, we shall in so doing be examining a final and most important aspect of children's work orientations.

As Lenski has succinctly put it, "The basic question to which all theories of stratification are addressed is *Who gets what and why?*"[3] Here, we have set for ourselves the task of exploring children's knowledge and beliefs in this regard. The goal is a broad one which will require our touching upon several closely related issues. We shall begin by inquiring in a most basic fashion into children's awareness of social class. Do children recognize the existence of differentials in terms of social status? Occupational prestige? Economic standing? If so, to what do they attribute such differences? Then, we shall turn our attention to a derivative question. To what degree does the child's awareness of social class serve as an organizing principle for other perceptions? Put differently, this question asks how salient is social class in the world-view of the child. Our efforts to answer that question will lead us to put to the test children's awareness of occupational stratification through the analysis of their knowledge of income differentials, in both absolute and relative terms.

Children's Perceptions of Social Class

The sociological literature suggests that children steadily grow into their awareness of social class. Stendler, for example, in her pioneering study on the subject noted that developmental changes are especially in evidence in the differences between first and fourth graders, that beyond grade six children exhibited "no striking differences" with respect to such awareness.[4] Elsewhere in the same work, she amended that slightly, stating that while there are signs throughout the elementary years of increasing agreement with adult views of social class, "The greatest growth in awareness took place between grade four and six.[5] Davies, who later reviewed the literature on children's discovery of social class, concluded that whatever one's "class scheme" (conception of the stratification system) it is likely both to be rooted in childhood experiences and to have developed very early in life, say by the end of childhood.[6]

Following such examples, we wished first to establish a baseline with respect to young children's knowledge of social class. To that end, we began our inquiry by asking children in grades one, three, and five[7] whether in their opinions some people are more important than others. Egalitarianism notwithstanding, it was clear that most pupils were cognizant of the fact that "importance" (which is to say "esteem" or "prestige") is differentially distributed. The results show that 73.5 percent (139), 77 percent (159), and 81 percent (167) of first, third, and fifth graders, respectively, responded in the affirmative to this item. Children's responses to this question did not vary significantly by grade in school. We interpret this not as a contradiction of Stendler's findings of developmental differences, but as the predictable outcome of our decision to ask a more basic question than had Stendler.[8]

Of greater interest, because they afford some insight into the "class schemes" held by children, are their responses to the logical next question, that of *why* most believe that some people are more important than others. Not unexpectedly, given the context of all our data collection efforts, children typically answered in terms of *jobs* rather than personalities. They commonly offered these sorts of explanations for prestige differentials.

First, many children alluded to the fact that some people perform work which is important to society, or have skills which are demanded by or benefit the community at large. "Yes, [some are more important if] their job is more helpful," was one third grader's assessment. "People who solve problems," were, in the eyes of another child, more important than others. Many answered by example, citing community reliance upon certain key positions (like those of physician, police officer, fire officer) which they considered essential. "If *they* didn't do stuff," reasoned a fifth grade boy, "it would be worse than if others didn't do stuff." These answers have in common that one's contribution to the good of the community is implicitly or explicitly the referent for the child's assessment. Let us call these *community-based functional* explanations.

Other children answered in a way which, to many, might be classifiable only as tautological or ritualistic. That is to say, they replied that some are more important because they have wealth, fame, power, or authority. Thus, it was not uncommon for a child to view certain persons as important "because they earn more money." Some people, "like the president or governor [are more important] because they're famous," replied an eight-year-old girl. A male classmate observed "certain people have power. That makes them more important." Such responses are in many respects tautological, to be sure. But they also reveal an awareness of what might be termed the *correlates of social class,* and we shall consider them in that light.

The third category of answer is predicated on the child's apparent assumption that hard work earns one the esteem of others. Many children equated important people with hard workers. "They do a lot more work," said one child of those he regarded as important. "Some people can do things better than somebody else," said a third grader, obviously cognizant of the dimension of quality. For lack of a better term, let us call these *Horatio Alger* explanations, since they refer principally to individual success rather than to contributions to the community.

Table 5.1 shows the distribution, by grade in school, of the three sorts of schemes plus "other" responses not codable in those terms. Two age trends are in evidence. First, the so-called community-based, functional account of inequality, while the modal category among first and third graders, declines in popularity at grade five. Second, answers expressed in terms of the correlates of social class show a steady rate of increase from grade one to five, ultimately becoming the most commonly-offered explanation. The increase in the proportion of these responses is apparently at the expense of all other categories of answers.

TABLE 5.1
Children's explanations for status differentials
by grade in school*

Why are some people more important?	Grade in school**		
	1st	3rd	5th
Community-based, functional explanations (some fill socially important roles)	38.8% (40)	40.5% (53)	28.0% (44)
Explanations in terms of correlates of status (wealth, power, authority, fame)	15.5 (16)	26.0 (34)	42.0 (66)
"Horatio Alger" explanations (some work harder)	27.2 (28)	19.1 (25)	17.8 (28)
Other explanations (extraneous)	18.5 (19)	14.5 (19)	12.1 (19)
Total cases:	103	131	157

$$(x^2 = 23.96 \qquad p < .001)$$

* Percentages based upon number of pupils who had previously answered that some people were more important and who furnished reasons for their opinions.

** Seventh graders were not asked this question.

No significant differences by sex, SES, or community of residence were found in children's responses to this question.

Insofar as assigning some meaning to these findings is concerned, the following observations may be offered. Social scientists since the days of Marx have shown enormous preoccupation with this question. As mentioned in an earlier chapter, sociologists have long been divided over such matters, falling roughly into two camps—those who believe that social inequality is "functional," and those who do not. The so-called functional theory of stratification, as propounded by Davis and Moore, holds that inequality is both necessary and inevitable, that it exists as "an unconsciously evolved device by which societies insure that the most important positions are conscientiously filled by the most qualified persons."[9] Motivation is in many respects the conceptual key to this theory, which assumes that talented people must be enticed to sacrifice in order to be trained for and competently occupy the positions which are most important to the society. The opportunity to gain disproportionate shares of valued social rewards (including money, leisure, prestige, and self-respect) serves as the carrot which keeps people motivated to behave in ways which are functional from the standpoint of the system.

Opposed to this are other sorts of explanations, usually more cynical in nature, which stress the *ideological* significance of social stratification. Marx, Engels, and the subsequent conflict theorists, for example, long before the functionalist theory was proposed, had noted that *false consciousness* involved the acceptance by the "have nots" of the version of reality offered by the "haves" in this regard.[10] In our own times, the most astute critic of the functional approach has been Tumin, who has insisted we not lose sight of the fact that: "Social stratification systems function to provide the elite with the political power necessary to procure acceptance and dominance of an ideology which rationalizes the *status quo* whatever it may be as 'logical,' 'natural,' and 'morally right.' "[11] In other words, we would do well to regard *all* such accounts of the origin of social inequality as myths,[12] and to recognize that whether they *give rise* to or merely give voice to popular conceptions is an open question.

To which myths, if any, do our young respondents subscribe? If we seek only fully articulted accounts of social inequality, our answer must of course be that children express *none*. If, on the other hand, we are content to look for the *seeds* of such ideological commitment, then the findings portrayed in Table 5.1 assume further significance. While no child provided an elaborate scheme, the most common explanation among first and third graders was what we have termed the community-based, functional view. That is to say, many of the youngest children formulated their answers in terms of societal or community needs, noting, for example, that everyone would suffer if certain essential roles went unfilled.[13] Many others, especially among first graders, apparently adhered to what we have called the Horatio Alger version, predicated on the assumption that prestige is earned by dint of hard work. It should be emphasized that this account is not altogether dissimilar to the first. Implicit in both is the notion that one earns esteem by enduring sacrifice or investing more time or energy in work than do others. The importance which accrues to such persons is presumably viewed by children as a payoff or reward purchased at a price. The two accounts differ principally in terms of whether the community or the individual serves as the point of reference. Together, these two accounts are offered by two-thirds of the first graders (66 percent, N=68) and a slightly smaller percentage of third graders (60 percent, N=78) who provided explanations of any sort.

Weinstein in a 1958 study of fourth, sixth and eighth graders' conceptions of prestige noted a pattern very similar to that reported here. Instead of differentiating between the two responses, as we have done thus far, however, he argued persuasively that *both* reflected a popular conception of the Davis-Moore notion of the "differential functional importance" of occupations. The difference, he insisted, lay only in the degree of sophistication involved in each. His interpretation was greatly influenced no doubt by the fact that he found what we have termed the Horatio Alger version most common among young children, apparently supplanted by more elaborate functional explanations which emerge with age.[14] Here, we found both more prevalent among the younger children in the sample, then fading somewhat with age.

That the proportion of fifth graders offering either of these related explanations drops off to less than half (46 percent, N=72) does not necessarily mean, however, that children abandon such ideological positions. In fact, one could argue just the opposite, that in the absence of evidence that children shift to an ideologically incompatible position one could as easily interpret the decline in such responses to mean that older children are more likely to take such accounts for granted, to view them, as Tumin put it, as "logical" or "natural," not requiring explanation.

One *could* take that position, but it would be purely speculative. A more conservative, but more easily substantiated alternative explanation is to interpret the observed shift in children's responses simply as evidence of their tendencies with age to become more aware of and vocal about the various *correlates* of social class, as we have termed them here. In support of such an interpretation we would point out that Stendler had noted that, with respect to the *symbols* of social class, full awareness apparently does not occur until *after* grade four, and that *growth* is particularly evident between grades four and six.[15] This pattern is consistent with the rules observed.

In sum, then, we infer from the age trends in children's answers here that: (1) even the youngest, for the most part, recognize the existence of prestige differentials; (2) while virtually none of them fully articulated a true "class scheme," perhaps the majority evidenced at least the rudiments of one; (3) the most commonly found rudimentary explanations of prestige differentials had much in common with the ideological views presumably dominant among adult Americans of the middle and working classes, namely that one earns esteem largely by filling roles regarded by the community as essential and/or by virtue of personal diligence; and (4) that with age the correlates of social class become more salient in children's views of the world.

In an earlier chapter, it was noted that children tend to idealize political authority.[16] Nowhere was this more clearly revealed than in children's answers to the question "Who is important?" Most children, as Table 5.2 shows, furnished two or more examples of categories of people they deemed important. Among the youngest children, nearly half elected to refer to subjective or interpersonal importance, naming parents, relatives, or friends as important to them, or to children. This sort of response—along with the "other" or extraneous responses[17]—diminished considerably with age as older children were more likely to answer *exclusively* in terms of occupational importance. Children's esteem for political officials (president, governor, senator, mayor, etc.) increased enormously from first to fifth grade, becoming the most prominent category of answers by a margin of better than two to one. Note, too, that younger children's tendencies to name persons in other, nonpolitical occupations (teachers, doctors, nurses, firemen, etc.) apparently gives way among fifth graders to the perceptions of the overriding importance of political authorities.

The variations by demographic categories in children's responses were for the most part minor in comparison with age differences. While sex differences were not in general substantial, boys were somewhat more apt than girls to designate police officers as important. Similarly, middle-class children more frequently included police officers than did working-class children. Also of interest is the fact that about one in seven working-class children said that ordinary working people were important, compared to only 6 percent (6) of middle-class children.

TABLE 5.2
Percentage of children designating certain categories of people as important by grade in school*

| Who is important?: | Grade in school** | | |
	1st	3rd	5th
Parents, relatives, friends	44.0% (55)	26.6% (38)	15.1% (25)
Political officials (elected)	14.4 (18)	50.3 (72)	84.3 (140)
Police	29.6 (37)	26.9 (38)	12.7 (21)
Persons in other occupations specifically named	68.0 (85)	83.2 (119)	40.4 (67)
Bosses	32.0 (40)	29.4 (42)	29.5 (49)
Rich/famous persons	8.0 (10)	11.9 (17)	10.2 (17)
Working folks	12.0 (15)	9.8 (14)	4.8 (8)
Others	35.2 (44)	18.2 (26)	16.9 (28)
Total cases:	125	143	166

*   Percentages based on number of children who had earlier said some persons were more important than others, and who responded when asked to specify who these persons were. Also, percentages add to more than 100% because most children furnished more than one answer.

** Seventh graders were not asked this question.

We asked the same children for their assessments as to who is *not* important. Here, fewer children were able to answer, and very few multiple answers were received. Altogether, the same children who had furnished from two to three answers apiece on the earlier item averaged slightly less than one answer here. The answers received were nonetheless somewhat disconcerting, including a large range of categories: the elderly, the poor, the sick, anyone not in a leadership role, anyone who is not famous, women, housewives, students, and criminals. The two most prominent answers, however, were "people who do not work" and "people like us" (common, ordinary citizens), which accounted for 21 percent (68) and 26 percent (85) of the answers. While the former category may be in large part due to the "halo effect" in that nearly all our questions had to do with work and workers, it still casts some doubt upon the generalizability of our

TABLE 5.3
Children's answers to "Are some jobs
better than others?"
by grade in school[18]

	Grade in school			
Are some jobs better?	1st	3rd	5th	7th
Don't know	7.7% (14)	2.6% (5)	2.8% (6)	---- (0)
No, all are equally important	22.4 (41)	15.0 (29)	4.6 (10)	14.3 (15)
Yes	69.9 (128)	82.4 (159)	92.5 (198)	85.7 (90)
Total cases:	183	193	214	105

$$(x^2 = 42.23 \qquad p < .001)$$

previously reported finding that children do not seem to deprecate idleness. Even more disturbing from the standpoint of *anomie* is the fact that so many youngsters perceive themselves and people like them as unimportant in the larger scheme of things. No differences were found by sex, SES, or community of residence in these findings.

While the findings presented to this point strongly suggest children's *general awareness* of prestige differentials, we also sought specific information as to children's evaluations of *occupational* prestige. For that reason, we asked children (including seventh graders) whether in their opinions some *jobs* were better than others. The results, displayed in Table 5.3, correspond quite closely to our earlier findings, which reinforces the impression that children are aware of prestige differentials. Such awareness, already high among first graders, showed evidence of further increase with age. It was not found to vary significantly by sex, SES, or community of residence.

TABLE 5.4
Children's reasons for opinions that
some jobs are "better"
by grade in school

Why are some jobs better?	Grade in school*			
	1st	3rd	5th	7th
Don't know	26.6% (34)	14.5% (23)	11.6% (23)	1.1% (1)
Some pay better	28.1 (36)	42.8 (68)	56.6 (112)	51.1 (46)
Some are easier	22.7 (29)	22.0 (35)	14.1 (28)	23.3 (21)
It is a matter of personal preference	11.7 (15)	12.6 (20)	9.6 (19)	14.4 (13)
Some benefit the community more than others	9.4 (12)	7.5 (12)	3.0 (6)	3.3 (3)
Other	1.6 (2)	0.6 (1)	5.0 (10)	6.7 (6)
Total cases:	128	159	198	90

$$(x^2 = 63.43 \qquad p < .001)$$

* Percentages based on number of pupils who had said yes to previous questions, i.e., that some jobs were better than others.

Next, those children who had answered in the affirmative were asked *why* in their opinion some jobs were better than others. While the question clearly calls for a value judgment, it does not specify the basis for it. It was of interest to note that most children this time apparently used the individual worker, rather than the community, as the point of reference for such evaluations. Note in Table 5.4, for example, that economic remuneration and degree of difficulty account for the majority of explanations offered. With age, pay apparently becomes more important to children, but the "easiness" of the job does not. Very few indicated that the good of the community figured in their thinking in this regard. Once again, sex, SES, and community were not found to be significantly related to children's answers.

Personal wealth is perhaps the most obvious aspect of social class. In any event, we found it to be a most tangible one in the estimation of our respondents. All were conversant with the terms "rich" and "poor," and most could at least speculate on such matters as *why* some people are rich and others poor, the symbols of wealth and poverty, and the life-style implications of personal wealth and the lack thereof.

We must begin with the observation that for the child, while "rich" and "poor" may have the same abstract meanings as they do for most adults, the empirical referents for these terms may be quite different. For many, rich and poor are *absolute* concepts, denoting the most extreme positions on a continuum referring to the ability to satisfy personal wants. Rich people, children variously told us, live in castles, palaces or mansions. They (or their chauffeurs) drive "*giant* cars, like Cadillacs." They have yachts, horses, tennis courts, expensive jewelry, fancy clothes, pockets bulging with paper money, even "*real* gold." Poor people, according to many children, not only lack such luxuries, they lack nearly everything. "Some kids don't have any house," said one third grader. Others noted that the poor live in shacks or boarded-up houses. "You have to beg for food.", said another, "You have no money. You wear rags. And you sleep on newspapers, with no pillows." A six-year-old boy observed: "You wouldn't have any food. Starved! And no money to buy things. Wooden beds are uncomfortable."

There were, of course, variations on such social definitions. For some, being poor meant being unable to *buy* things, but not necessarily doing without them. "You don't have much money [if you are poor]. So you have to hunt food. You shoot rabbits, deer, squirrels, chipmunks," said a first grader. "You can't buy anything," said another, "You gotta make your own clothing and your own cars." For others, poverty apparently evokes images of foreign lands. "Some boys and girls die. This is in India, not all over," noted a third grade boys. "Well, in Mexico they [the poor] sit around the churches asking people for money. My uncle's in India, and probably *everybody* is begging him," said a first-grade boy. A few, of course, do recognize the relativism of such terms. "It matters *how* poor," said a third grade girl when asked what it was like to be poor, "If you're *really* poor, you sleep in a basket and don't have any food. If you're just *poor,* you don't have all the things which a rich person does."

Some children, in defining the terms "rich" and "poor," did not stop at merely noting the absence of money or even the inability to buy desired goods or enjoy certain services. They also alluded to the behavioral or psychological implications involved, i.e., they described wealthy people as happy, and poor people (especially children) as constantly sad, having no opportunities for fun.

TABLE 5.5
Criteria employed by children in assessing
social class differentials
by grade in school

	Grade in school*			
How can you tell if some- one is rich or poor?	1st	3rd	5th	7th
Don't know or no way to tell	16.8% (32)	3.0% (6)	3.7% (8)	2.8% (3)
By their clothing	21.1 (40)	73.0 (146)	74.5 (164)	94.5 (103)
By their homes or furnishings	13.2 (25)	39.5 (79)	23.6 (52)	45.9 (50)
By their other possessions (especially cars)	22.6 (43)	16.2 (32)	12.2 (27)	26.6 (29)
By their spending habits or displays of money	17.9 (34)	5.0 (10)	5.5 (12)	8.3 (8)
By facial expressions or demeanor	15.3 (29)	6.5 (13)	5.9 (13)	29.4 (32)
Other	14.7 (28)	16.0 (32)	15.9 (35)	10.1 (11)
Total cases:	190	200	220	109

* Percentages may add to more than 100% because many children furnished more than one response.

As Stendler noted, ". . . each social class has symbols which are recognized in many parts of the country."[19] In order to ascertain the extent of our respondents' awareness of such symbols, and the nature of the criteria involved in their perceptions of social class, we asked children *how they could tell* whether someone was rich or poor. As Table 5.5 shows, most children offered at least one observation on this subject. Only one first grader in six (and virtually none of the older children) either claimed he or she did not know how to tell or that there is no way to tell. Most referred to class-related differences in clothing, or in housing or furnishings. Other possessions, observable spending habits, even personal expressions or demeanor were also commonly employed by children as criteria for assessing social class differences. Clearly, Stendler's conclusions that awareness increased rapidly with age is supported here.

TABLE 5.6
Children's explanations of wealth/poverty differentials
by grade in school

Why are some rich others poor?	Grade in school			
	1st	3rd	5th	7th
Don't know	19.0% (36)	8.1% (16)	4.7% (10)	1.9% (2)
Work-related explanations	46.0 (87)	65.0 (128)	69.6 (149)	72.2 (78)
Result of fate, inheritance	9.0 (17)	11.7 (23)	21.5 (46)	22.2 (24)
Result of saving/ spending habits	11.6 (22)	8.6 (17)	1.4 (3)	6.5 (7)
Other	14.3 (27)	6.6 (13)	2.8 (6)	14.8 (16)
Total cases:	189	197	214	108

* Seventh grade percentages add to more than 100% because several multiple answers were recorded.

In the world of the child, being rich is thought to be mainly a function of whether and/or how hard one works. Similarly, to many children, being poor is most often due to not working, or to not working hard enough. As Table 5.6 clearly shows, work-related explanations of wealth and poverty dominated children's responses to the question "Why are some rich and others poor?" With age, children were more likely to express opinions on the subject. A few younger children gave "fantasy" answers (coded here as "fate") having to do with finding treasure or winning the lottery, and some indicated that personal savings/spending habits were important. In the case of the latter, younger children tended to be negativistic, i.e., to say that people become poor by squandering all their money. They rarely mentioned accumulating wealth through savings. With age, children were slightly more likely to indicate a different sort of fateful answer, namely that rich people are born into wealthy families or inherit their wealth. While this answer became more prominent, the work-related explanations were clearly dominant at all grade levels.

In summary of this section, it may be said with considerable justification that even the youngest children exhibited *at least* a rudimentary awareness of social class differences in the world. Most, for example, were cognizant of differences among people in terms of "importance," i.e., esteem of prestige. Most were even able to offer explanations as to why this was the case. In analyzing those explanations, we observed the seeds of the more popular explanations for social inequality found among American adults, and we noted the steady increase with age in children's tendencies to speak of what we have called correlates of social class—wealth, power, authority, fame, etc.

When asked to specify exactly *who* is important, children as we have seen, tended to answer in occupational terms. With age, this tendency became stronger, virtually precluding all other sorts of answers. Moreover, political officials were particularly esteemed, especially among the older children sampled. On the other side of the coin, the question of who is *not* important elicited some rather disturbing answers from many children: non-workers and "people like us." The former may be an artifact of our persistent line of work-oriented questioning, but the latter may be regarded as a source of concern, an early indicant of the seeds of political *anomie*.

When we asked whether some *jobs* (as opposed to some *people*) are better than others, the general response pattern corroborated our earlier observation of children's awareness of social class. The issue of *better for whom* was intentionally left to the child, however, and we found children more likely to be thinking along personal rather than community-based lines in this regard. That is to say, most said that the better jobs were those which paid best and/or were easy. Children's awareness of social class, not unexpectedly, extended to the issue of personal wealth. "Rich" and "poor" had meaning for all children, although often in a rather absolute and limited sense compared to adult conceptions. And, we were able to corroborate Stendler's observation that awareness of the *symbols* of social class (clothing, houses, cars, even behavioral/psychological traits) are increasingly known to children as they grow older, but certainly well understood by the end of elementary school. Being rich or poor was apparently looked upon by most children as largely a function of one's personal work-related efforts, although there was some evidence of awareness of the role played by birth in the process. Finally, we must note that such demographic variables as sex, SES, and community of residence were relatively insignificant in terms of their impact upon children's awareness of social class.

Class Awareness as a Principle of Perceptual Organization

Having established children's awareness of social class, let us turn our attention to what is perhaps a more important question, namely that of the *relevance* of social class in the world of the child. As Weinstein has pointed out, by internalizing and learning to respond to the conception of a general hierarchy, the individual is learning a role of sorts—that of an ascriber of prestige.[20] We know from the findings reported thus far that most children had the dimension of social class *available* to them as a criterion for other perceptions. Here, we would like to establish the extent to which they relied upon it as an organizing principle for their perceptions. To this end, we shall pursue two related lines of inquiry. First, we shall review very briefly some of the "sorting" data presented in an earlier chapter, this time with an eye toward what they tell us with respect to the salience of social class in the child's scheme of the world of work. Then—and of greater interest to us here—we shall examine children's estimates of occupational income (both in relative and absolute terms) in search of further inferences regarding the significance of social class in their views of such matters.

In Chapter 2 we presented data concerning the reports of children in grades three, five, and seven about the criteria employed in their sorting decisions with respect to some thirty-three diverse occupations. Recall, for example, that role partnership, situs, and specific activities were the most frequently cited common denominators among the sixteen dimensions which occurred with any regularity. Now, on the basis of findings presented earlier in this chapter we may conclude that the majority of children *could* indeed have employed social class in their sorting decisions, had it seemed relevant to them to do so. In fact, three such indicants of social class awareness were found among the criteria actually furnished by children: status/

prestige, ownership/capital, income/wealth. Of these, however, only status/prestige recurred very frequently, and it ranked a distant fifth on the list, having been employed by only 12 percent (21), 19 percent (41), and 11 percent (16) of third, fifth, and seventh graders respectively. Ownership/capital ranked thirteenth and the income/wealth dimension ranked sixteenth and last. Thus, we must observe that although children are aware of social class, it certainly does not arise spontaneously as an important factor in their views of the similarities or differences among occupations. To most children, it would seem, occupations are principally arrayed according to activity, situs, or role partnership, not position within the perceived occupational hierarchy.

Again, sex, SES, and community of residence made virtually no difference in the observed pattern of findings with respect to children's sorting behavior.

Several investigators have employed a very different sort of strategy in studying children's awareness of social class. Such studies start with what is known about adult behavior in ascribing prestige to occupations, often using the North-Hatt or NORC[21] findings as a norm for assessing children's rankings of the same occupations. Then, the strategy is a simple one—children are furnished a list of occupations, the adult rankings of which are known; after the children rank them in order of imputed prestige, this set of rankings is then correlated with those of adults. The resultant coefficient of rank-order correlation, since it measures the goodness of fit between children's perceptions and those of adults, is taken as an indication of the levels of children's awareness of social class and occupational hierarchies. Of particular interest in this regard are studies by Weinstein,[22] Simmons,[23] Gunn,[24] Simmons and Rosenberg,[25] and Lauer.[26] While those studies varied in terms of the grade levels of children tested (ranging from second to twelfth grade), they typically had in common findings of extremely high rank-order correlations between children's rankings and those of adults. Taken together, these studies argue quite convincingly that children's awareness of social class is operational by the early years of elementary school and increases quite rapidly, until it approximates adult levels by perhaps eighth grade.

This is not to suggest, however, that children employ the same reasoning in their ranking decisions at every age, or that the criteria they use are identical to those employed by adults. Weinstein, for example, insisted that children's thinking in this regard is in a state of flux and does not always approximate adult reasoning.[27] Simmons agreed, and in fact found virtually *no* relationship between the *criteria* employed by fourth and twelfth graders in their ranking decisions, despite the fact that their rankings themselves were substantially in agreement. He suggested that eighth grade represents a "transitional period" during which such reasoning has much in common with both the childish criteria of the fourth grader and the adult views of the high school senior.[28]

Here, our interest lies in exploring the extent to which awareness of social class shapes children's other perceptions. To achieve this end, we examined children's estimates, not of prestige, but of occupational *income*—a factor closely related to prestige, but not previously explored in any systematic way in the literature on childhood socialization. First, income is more tangible to children; it requires fewer assumptions about their abilities to do abstract thinking. Second is the readily quantifiable nature of the variable, which enables the researcher to assess quite easily the rewards a child thinks an occupation merits, not only in *relative* terms, but in *absolute* dollar values as well. This last fact assumes great significance in that it allows us to speak with greater certainty about the degree of *realism* involved in the child's awareness of occupational incomes. For example, a child who believes that a physician earns $100 per year may be regarded as *less realistic* than one who estimates $10,000. Finally, income estimates, like prestige estimates, may be judged against an objective, empirical standard (in this case, the U.S. Census estimates of median incomes by selected occupations)[29] and even rank-ordered and correlated with that standard.

We begin with our findings about the absolute values of children's income estimates. Children were asked to make their "best guess" as to the annual incomes of ten occupational categories ranging from the president to janitor and waitress. Four of the occupations were typically occupied by females, six by males. In interview situations (first and third grade) the list of occupations was presented in random order by the interviewer. In written administrations of the instrument[30] (fifth and seventh grade), children were presented with a two-column list of the ten occupations. Table 5.7 shows the computed median income estimates (rounded to the nearest dollar) by age and sex of our respondents.

Two things are obvious from this table: (1) in terms of the accuracy of their estimates of the absolute values associated with selected occupational incomes, children clearly advance quite rapidly during the elementary years; and (2) realism or accuracy comes somewhat sooner for the boys than the girls.[31] Note for example that with the exception of the president (thought to earn $100 or $200) not a single occupation was estimated by first grade boys or girls (as a group) to have an average *annual* income which exceeds double figures. Clearly, first and third graders of either sex or not even "in the ballpark" in terms of their grasp of the absolute dollar value dimension of occupational incomes. By fifth grade, however, the estimates—especially those of the boys—assume more reasonable proportions. Girls, while in some instances prone to somewhat lower estimates, also become dramatically more realistic with age, and by grade seven must also be regarded as reasonably well-informed on such matters.

TABLE 5.7
Children's computed median annual income estimates
for selected occupations
by grade in and sex

Occupation:	1st		3rd		5th		7th	
	Boys	Girls	Boys	Girls	Boys	Girls	Boys	Girls
Secretary	$ 50	$ 30	$300	$300	$5,001	$1,145	$10,000	$5,025
Truck driver	35	30	601	300	7,000	1,021	11,000	7,800
Banker	81	61	999	900	9,003	3,000	13,548	12,000
Policeman	70	50	900	400	7,500	5,000	11,995	11,983
President	200	100	3,002	1,000	100,004	40,003	99,344	100,167
Doctor	50	41	701	400	20,000	5,000	23,148	29,985
Janitor	50	40	201	150	2,998	1,001	6,002	4,000
Waitress	31	40	200	200	2,089	1,000	7,000	3,000
Teacher	30	30	300	210	6,997	3,000	12,999	12,123
Nurse	50	31	500	400	10,000	4,000	12,031	10,013
Total cases:	84	62	88	73	72	82	48	33

Controlling by grade and SES,[32] we found that the same general age-related pattern of increasing realism obtains, but in grades three, five, and seven middle-class children's estimates tended to be slightly higher than those of working class children.

Can we conclude, given the wholly unrealistic nature of the annual income estimates provided by first and third graders, that these children are less aware of occupational income differentials, or merely that they have no grasp of relatively large numbers or long periods of time? In order to shed some light on this issue, every fifth child[33] in the sample was asked to furnish *weekly* rather than annual estimates of the incomes in question. As Table 5.8 shows, the weekly estimates of these first and third graders, while somewhat lower than the annual estimates of their age mates, were in the same generally unrealistic, understated range. Fifth and seventh graders' weekly estimates, on the other hand, were correspondingly "scaled down" in comparison to the annual estimates of their age mates, and no less accurate. The point we wish to make here is merely that such findings corroborate our earlier observation about the unrealistic nature of first and third graders' estimates. Indeed, such findings suggest that many children at these age levels are practically without foundation in terms of their abilities to estimate the *absolute values* of occupational incomes.

TABLE 5.8
Children's computed median weekly income estimates for selected occupations by grade in school*

Occupation:	Estimates			
	1st	3rd	5th	7th
Secretary	$ 9	$ 75	$100	$198
Truck driver	18	90	200	283
Banker	20	120	230	250
Policeman	16	100	200	221
President	70	800	999	1,500
Doctor	13	109	351	501
Janitor	10	51	99	125
Waitress	11	51	100	101
Teacher	10	90	146	195
Nurse	10	96	200	200
Total cases:	40	44	50	25

* Based on a one-in-five subsample of all children furnishing income estimates.

This last point—that most first graders and third graders have no apparent grasp of the *absolute* dollar values associated in reality with occupational incomes—becomes extremely interesting in light of our subsequent findings concerning these children's awareness of the *relative* distribution of income by occupation. Unlike the studies cited earlier, we did not ask children to *rank* these occupations, merely to furnish an income estimate for each. Thereafter, our coders ranked each child's raw estimates in order of their magnitude, taking into account tied estimates. Next, these data were aggregated in such a fashion that it became possible to state, for example, the order in which first grade girls, given their previous estimates, typically ranked these occupations in terms of income. Rank-order correlation coefficients (Kendall's *tau*)[34] were then computed versus the rankings of these occupations as compiled on the basis of actual census estimates of median incomes for persons in those occupations.[35] Table 5.9 shows these rank-order correlations by grade and sex.

TABLE 5.9
Rank-order correlation coefficients (Kendall's *tau*)
between census data rankings, for selected
occupations and children's rankings
by grade and sex*

	Kendall's tau	Significance (p<)	Cases (N=)
1st graders			
Boys	.449	.05	84
Girls	.378	.07	62
3rd graders			
Boys	.733	.01	88
Girls	.689	.01	73
5th graders			
Boys	.778	.001	72
Girls	.733	.01	82
7th graders			
Boys	.809	.001	48
Girls	.604	.01	33

*   Based on rankings of annual estimates only.

The most obvious conclusions to be drawn from these findings are: (1) that awareness of occupational income differentials increases rapidly during the elementary years until it is quite realistic indeed; and (2) that girls, while also clearly experiencing growth in awareness, tend to lag behind boys in this regard. Since, however, the correlations upon which these conclusions are based are ultimately a function of the raw dollar estimates of the children, we cannot claim that our findings here corroborate patterns established previously, merely that they restate them in slightly different form.

The real significance of the correlational analysis here may be seen in the juxtaposition of two findings. First, the rank order correlations between first graders' rankings and those of the actual census data, while not exceedingly high, nonetheless suggest that first graders are not wholly unrealistic in terms of their awareness of the *relative* distributions of income by occupation. Among third graders, the rank-order correlations are such that realism must be considered very high. In fact, the rankings by third grade boys themselves correlated quite highly with those of seventh grade boys (*tau* = .719, p < .01). Similarly, third and seventh grade girls' estimates yielded rankings which closely approximated one another (*tau* = .733, p < .01). In short, in terms of their awareness of the *relative* distribution of occupational incomes, even the younger children must for the most part be regarded as on solid ground. And yet, it must be emphasized, the same rankings which lead to these conclusions are themselves based upon *absolute value* income estimates which, for first and third graders, are absurdly inaccurate in comparison to the real world. Put in terms of an example, these data suggest that even many first graders who might have thought, say, that a truck driver earns $40 annually, would nonetheless have estimated, no matter how inaccurate that first figure proved, that the doctor and the banker earn *more,* while the waitress and the janitor earn *less.*

Such a finding, unless accompanied by a more ultimate explanation, would indeed be anamalous. However, there is an explanation which we submit renders these findings plausible. It is possible that, just as our coders were basing their rankings upon children's income estimates, the children were actually basing their income estimates upon a *previously internalized* notion of an occupational ranking system. That is, they may have already been familiar with the relative statuses of these occupations and, having offered their first estimate, had only to scale their subsequent estimates to it, placing them higher or lower accordingly. Thus, if one "knew" a policeman ranked higher than a secretary it would hardly matter what incomes one assigned to each, so long as the estimate for the police officer was higher. In support of this position, we offer further correlational analysis, this time between children's *weekly* and *annual* estimates. Among first graders, the rank-order correlation between the aggregated rankings for children's weekly estimates versus those for annual estimates was high (*tau* = .689, p < .01). Among third graders, the two sets of rankings were practically *identical* (*tau* = .944, p < .0001). Such findings suggest quite convincingly that it is the relative status of occupations, and not the magnitude of the incomes associated with them, upon which children rely in assessing such matters. In short, their awareness of social class is apparently in place and operational by the early years of elementary school and in some respects serves as an organizing principle for their other perceptions.

Summary and Conclusions

Ours is a stratified society in which most of us learn "our places" in relation to those of other status holders. No matter what myths we perpetuate about equality, informal means of ranking are constantly employed in everyday living. Classifications according to social class or status are important criteria for making judgments and setting expectation levels with regard to both strangers and acquaintances.

Ordinarily such rankings are arrived at informally at least in part on the basis of occupational groupings and income levels. Such crude generalizations as "He's a doctor," and "She earns $3,700 a year," have wider connotative meanings: They serve for many of us as clues as to *who* people are, what to expect of them, how they live, etc.

Here, we have sought information on children's social definitions of esteem/prestige and social status and their allocation in society. We have sought children's "class schemes" in their perceptions of the rationales for differentials in esteem and wealth. And we have explored the extent to which they rely upon their awareness of social class in, for example, their classification of occupations and their estimations of occupational income differentials. While our findings have not been wholly consistent—we found social class to be of relatively little import in children's sorting behavior—they have for the most part corroborated one another to produce the notion that, *with respect to their awareness of social class, children live in more or less the same world as do adults*. We must qualify that somewhat, for we have concentrated here upon their perceptions, not class-related feelings. But the general impression conveyed by our findings is one of children as relatively well informed, or at least not unlike adults in this respect, often by the early years of elementary school.

Notes

1. George Orwell, *Animal Farm* (New York: Harcourt, Brace and World, Inc. 1946), p. 148.
2. For our purposes, social stratification refers to the systematic differential distribution among individuals of the scarce and/or valued resources a society has to offer. Those resources or "rewards," as they are sometimes considered, typically are thought to include power, wealth, and social honor (status or prestige).

3.   Gerhard Lenski, "A Theoretical Synthesis," in *Social Stratification: A Reader,* ed. Joseph Lopreato and Lionel S. Lewis (New York: Harper and Row, 1974), p. 75. See also: Gerhard Lenski, *Power and Privilege* (New York: McGraw-Hill, 1966).

4.   Celia B. Stendler, *Children of Brasstown* (Urbana, Ill.: University of Illinois Press, 1949), pp. 37-40.

5.   Ibid., p. 72.

6.   A. F. Davies, "The Child's Discovery of Social Class," *The Australian and New Zealand Journal of Sociology* 1 (April 1965), pp. 21-37.

7.   First and third graders were interviewed; fifth graders responded in writing. Seventh graders were not asked this question, as pre-tests of the instruments showed that many considered the answer so obvious as not to require a reply.

8.   Stendler, for example, employed her "Guess Who" test in which children were to classify classmates in terms of the likelihood of their being associated with certain symbols, traits, or behaviors often considered indicative of class membership. Our question here is clearly much less demanding.

9.   Kingsley Davis and Wilbert E. Moore, "Some Principles of Stratification," *American Sociological Review* 10 (April 1945), pp. 242-249.

10.   As Marx put it, "The ideas of the ruling class are, in every age, the ruling ideas: i.e., the class which is the dominant material force in society is at the same time its dominant intellectual force." See: Karl Marx, *Selected Writings in Sociology and Social Philosophy,* trans. T. B. Bottomore (New York: McGraw-Hill, 1956), p. 78.

11.   Melvin M. Tumin, "Some Principles of Stratification: A Critical Analysis," *American Sociological Review,* 18 (August 1953), pp. 387-394.

12.   For our purposes here, characterizing an account as a "myth" is not intended as a commentary upon the truth of the account. Rather, a myth refers to a prevailing idea, the truth of which is irrelevant, which serves as a guiding principle or rationale for other beliefs and/or actions.

13.   Note the similarity of this reasoning to that of Davis and Moore:

> But actually it does make a great deal of difference who gets into which positions, not only because some positions are inherently more agreeable than others, but also because some require special talents or training and some are functionally more important than others.

See: Davis and Moore, "Some Principles of Stratification," pp. 242-249.

14.   Eugene A. Weinstein, "Children's Conceptions of Occupational Stratification," *Sociology and Social Research,* 42 (March-April 1958), pp. 278-284.

15.   Stendler, *Children of Brasstown,* pp. 90-92.

16.   See Chapter II.

17.   By "extraneous" here we mean answers not readily codable into the categories established. For example, some children said God, Jesus, holy people, kings, queens, children, even pets were important.

18. First, third, and fifth graders answered the question as posed in the Man-From-Mars Series, Form C. Seventh graders answered the question as posed in the Knowledge of Work Questionnaire, Part I. This is also true for Tables 5.4, 5, and 6.

19. Stendler, *Children of Brasstown,* p. 16.

20. Eugene Weinstein, "Weights Assigned by Children to Criteria of Prestige," *Sociometry* 19 (June 1956), pp. 126-132.

21. This scale lists in order of their "social standing" in the eyes of a nationwide sample some ninety occupations. See: National Opinion Research Center, "Jobs and Occupations: A Popular Evaluation" *Opinion News* 9 (September 1947), pp. 3-13. For an expanded and critical look at the NORC scale, in terms of both substance and methodology, see: Albert J. Reiss, Jr., Otis Dudly Duncan, Paul K. Hatt, and Cecil C. North, *Occupations and Social Status* (Glencoe, Ill.: Free Press, 1961).

22. Weinstein, "Weights Assigned by Children."

23. Dale D. Simmons, "Children's Rankings of Occupational Prestige," *Personnel and Guidance Journal* 41 (December 1962), pp. 332-336.

24. Barbara Gunn, "Children's Conceptions of Occupational Prestige," *Personnel and Guidance Journal* 42 (February 1964), pp. 558-563.

25. Roberta G. Simmons and Morris Rosenberg, "Functions of Children's Perceptions of the Stratification System," *American Sociological Review* 36 (April 1971), pp. 235-249.

26. Robert H. Lauer, "Socialization into Inequality: Children's Perceptions of Occupational Status," *Sociology and Social Research* 50 (January 1974), pp. 176-183.

27. Weinstein, "Weights Assigned by Children."

28. Dale D. Simmons, "Children's Rankings."

29. U.S. Department of Commerce, Bureau of the Census, *Money Income in 1971 of Families and Persons in the United States,* Series p-60, no. 85 (Washington, D.C.: U.S. Government Printing Office, 1972).

30. Children in grades one, three, and five were administered Form D of the Man-From-Mars Series. Fifth graders responded in writing to the same questions asked in the Knowledge of Work Questionnaire, Part II.

31. In this sense, the pattern observed here corresponded to that noted by Simmons, who found the boys' prestige rankings substantially agreed with those of adults (i.e., had rank order correlations in the .80's) by fourth grade, whereas for girls such agreement typically came by eighth grade. See: Dale D. Simmons, "Children's Rankings."

32. Because the N's became very small, we did not, in examining children's estimates by grade and SES, control for sex.

33. More precisely, this subsample actually turned out to be 23 percent (N=159) of the respondents to these instruments.

34. While most of the literature involving correlations between children's and adults' rankings of occupational prestige use Spearman's *rho* rank-order correlation coefficient, the relatively high incidence of ties in these data suggested the advisability of the use of Kendall's *tau,* which is more readily computed if there are ties in the data, and equally powerful in terms of rejecting the null hypothesis. See: Sidney Siegel, *Nonparametric Statistics for the Behavioral Sciences* (New York:

McGraw-Hill, 1956), pp. 213-223. See also: Hubert M. Blalock, *Social Statistics* (New York: McGraw-Hill, 1960), pp. 319-324.

35.   The income *rankings* of the ten occupations in question, on the basis of actual census estimates of median annual incomes for persons in those occupational categories, were (in descending order) as follows: president (not reported in census), doctor (M.D.), bank officer, police officer, truck driver, teacher, janitor, nurse, secretary, and waitress.

Chapter 6

Children's Conception of Work:
An Overview

In previous chapters, we presented rather specific and detailed accounts of four major aspects of children's work orientations. Our task in this chapter is to recapitulate and integrate the findings in an effort to achieve some measure of generalization, and to assign some meanings to the finding.

Children and Work: A General Summary

While there have been numerous studies in the literature on political socialization, as well as relevant studies in psychology and education, a comprehensive investigation of orientations to work in childhood necessarily took us into relatively uncharted areas of inquiry. Thus, we took it upon ourselves to offer an overview of the topic, in contrast to final hypothesis-testing regarding children and their conception of work. Put differently, our major goal in this study has been to outline the parameters of the problem of children's orientation in this sphere.

The resultant mapping of this area of inquiry may be divided, perhaps arbitrarily, into four principal areas: (1) children's baseline knowledge of the world of work; (2) their commitment to work; (3) their work-related affective states and tendencies to employ stereotypes in their occupational thinking; and (4) their awareness of social class as it relates to work. We shall recapitulate the findings in each of these substantive areas in as concise a manner, emphasizing such generalizations as are possible. Thereafter, we shall turn to the question of the impact of certain key demographic variables upon children's orientations to work.

In Chapter 2, the overarching question concerned cognition. An attempt was made to ascertain the "child's eye view" of the world of work. Analysis of the consistent age-related decline in children's "Don't know" responses suggested that while even first graders grasped more than many of us would presumably have given them credit for, there was strong evidence that children's knowledge of basic economic concepts and relationships was governed by a developmental process. In the earliest grades tested, it was often clear that even though certain concepts were available to children in their recognition vocabularies, cognitions were often limited to fantasy-based misconceptions and gross oversimplifications. However, conceptual understanding was found in most instances to advance rapidly. By fifth grade most children evidenced sophisticated comprehension of occupations.

This general pattern of age-related growth obtained for the most part with respect to children's social definitions of work and its significance in both social and individual life. While the trend could hardly be called dramatic, it was nonetheless clear that the elementary years of schooling provided the setting for a shift in children's thinking with respect to work. During this period egocentric and concretistic views give way *to a degree* to more abstract and objective accounts of the economic and social significance of work.

More specific inquiries into children's knowledge of such phenomena as "getting jobs," pay differentials, and occupational authority, indicated results in keeping with the previously-observed pattern. Thus, our findings strongly supported the contention that *realism* increases demonstrably throughout the elementary years. The findings concerning children's knowledge of labor disputes and the welfare system are especially interesting; they suggest the existence of "threshhold effects" in pupils' awareness of these phenomena. That is to say, it appears that most fifth graders evidence a "readiness" for certain work-related concepts uncommonly manifest among third graders. If asked to identify a critical age or water-shed period in children's development of occupational awareness, it would appear that the fifth grade is crucial.

Knowledge of parental occupational activity, perhaps because it is so readily available to the child at the interpersonal (rather than cultural) level, proved an exception to this pattern. First graders varied widely in terms of their levels of information about such matters; however, children in grades above the first were equally aware of the occupational activities of working parents of both sexes. This finding is deceptive, since the research instruments were geared toward quantification of children's answers, and are less sensitive to qualitative variations in the depth of children's awareness of occupations. Perhaps then it is better to state this result more cautiously: While the range among first graders in knowledge of parental work roles varies considerably, children in the third, fifth, and seventh grades tended to differ in much more subtle fashions; virtually all children have a moderate awareness of parents' work.

However, children not only see and hear about work, most of them experience it first-hand through their performance of chores and so-called "childwork." Regrettably, it has not been possible in the present investigation to determine the impact of children's work experiences upon their work-related cognition states. But the evidence suggests that children's work and earning experiences (1) typically start in early childhood on a *very* small scale; (2) are extremely widespread; and (3) apparently are subjected to age-related increments. With respect to experiential factors, however, seventh grade, rather than fifth, represents a turning point, probably for reasons which have more to do with structural and physical considerations than with any appreciable change in children's readiness or willingness to work at that age. In any event, it is not until the last years of elementary school that we find extensive, regular performance of childwork outside the family to be widespread.

Chapter 3 investigated children's attachment to the social institution of work, in particular their commitment to the work ethic. Although it was neither possible nor completely desirable to divorce evaluative from cognitive issues, the emphasis was intended to be upon the former. While the results concerning values were not nearly so clearcut as had been earlier findings concerning purely cognitive matters, it was nonetheless possible to discern the prevalence of an "imperfect" version of the Protestant Ethic among the children sampled. While most children indicated essentially positive feelings about working, few could be said to predicate their "attachment" upon any intrinsic satisfaction they expected to derive from work. Rather, most apparently view work as a means to an end, i.e., making money. Although such findings give one pause, considering their potential implications for children's predisposition for worker alienation in the future, at present there is no way of knowing how much significance to attach to them. Certainly many children at the very least have come to the realization that adults very often dislike work; it is even possible that some feel constrained by norms which suggest that as one ages, one *ought to* dislike work. And yet the great majority of children were found to be overwhelmingly positive about *their own* work experiences. Results were also mixed with respect to other indicants of internalization of the work ethic. Given the opportunity to disparge idleness in their evaluations of non-workers, practically all children sampled refrained from doing so. Upward mobility aspirations figured prominently in the occupational thinking of most, but hardly all, children. Most children reported saving money; some even specified long-range saving goals which seemingly point to the existence of the tendency to defer gratification. Considering that our subjects were children, a prudent generalization based upon these findings would be that at least the *seeds* of the work ethic have been implanted in most of these youth. Whether it is reasonable to expect such value configurations to blossom or to atrophy, we cannot say. *In any event, it is clear that nothing in these findings warrants our mourning the death of the work ethic, at least not at this time, among these children of middle- and working-class families.*

In chapter 4, the focal issues were children's work-related feelings and the role played by stereotypes in their occupational thinking. Again, it has not been entirely possible to separate effect from perceptions. Not surprisingly, work did not compare favorably to play in the child's scheme of things. Work elicited feelings and/or images of pain, difficulty, involuntary or constraining activity, etc. Only a minority of children felt that people *like* to work. With age, however, children were more likely to have more complex views, i.e., to realize that such feelings were contingent upon personality factors and job characteristics. Interestingly, we again noted the existence of a double standard in which children, while often of the opinion that most people feel negatively about work, indicated that they themselves like work. Concern was expressed about the potential for self-fulfilling prophecies to emerge and (needlessly) taint children's future work satisfactions. It was suggested that parents and others involved in the occupational socialization process not lose sight of the suggestibility of the child in this regard.

While stereotypes are cognitive structures, a case can also be made that they are often quite closely associated with feelings, especially when questions of identity are involved. After first establishing the existence of predictable variations by sex in first graders' affective reactions to sex-typed occupations, we turned our attention to assessing the impact of stereotypical imagery upon children's occupational orientations. Impressionistic and essentially qualitative data were examined to elicit evidence of the nature and strength of the role played by stereotyping in children's evaluations of occupational role performance. By presenting children with illustrations of violated occupational sex-role stereotypes, it was possible to note numerous instances in which their reactions suggest (1) that such imagery is often quite strong indeed; and (2) that stereotypes (or specifically, their violation) readily arouse value judgments and affective states among children. Such findings demand replication before their meaning may be precisely assessed. Yet, in conjunction with other findings in the chapter, such results add to the impression that children are affectively involved in work-related issues, often through the perceptual mechanism of the stereotype. Suffice it to say, that children were found to be quite traditionalistic in their sex-typing behavior.

Chapter V returned to purely cognitive matters, taking up the issue of children's awareness of social class in relation to work. These findings clearly corroborated the much discussed notion that elementary children are aware of differentials by social class. And support was found for the contention that, with age, children's knowledge of the symbols of social status increased. Moreover, examination of children's beliefs with respect to the reasons for status differentials revealed the seeds of ideological commitment to the rationalization of the status quo. While children's beliefs in this regard increased in sophistication with age, we would not contend that a fully articulated "class scheme" is typically internalized by the latter years of elementary school, merely that the rudiments of one seem to be in their minds.

In terms of the categories of persons considered important in children's views, political authorities head the list, and that lead increases with the age of the children sampled.

Awareness of the concepts of wealth and poverty apparently develops early, and very often extends beyond knowledge of material possessions to include ideas about life-style, demeanor, even happiness. With age, children are increasingly likely to perceive linkages between such phenomena and the issue of personal wealth. It is clear that among children, being rich or poor is typically considered a function of personal industriousness: notions of birth, inheritance, situational factors, even luck (while sometimes present) apparently do not figure prominently in comparison with work-related explanations.

Having concluded the generally widespread existence among children of a functional, if not sophisticated, awareness of social class, we turned our attention finally to a related question, namely the extent to which children rely upon such awareness as an organizing principal for their perceptions. Our findings were of a mixed but interesting nature. On the one hand, analysis of children's sorting behavior suggested that, left to their own devices, children did not spontaneously impose the issue of social class upon occupational categories. On the other hand, the evidence that they *could* have done so—quite accurately and from a very early age—was indeed compelling. This last observation derives from analysis of the results of the income estimates furnished by children for ten selected occupations. While the realism of such estimates increased dramatically with age, there was little doubt that the youngest children simply had little or no grasp of the absolute dollar values associated with such incomes and/or of the time span encompassed by an annual estimate. Yet, when their raw income estimates were themselves ranked, aggregated and correlated with actual census rankings, it was clear that even the youngest children sampled must typically have had a working knowledge of the relative positions of occupations along some abstract status hierarchy. With age, correlations improved to the point at which children must be regarded as comparable to adults with respect to their knowledge of such matters.

If pressed to summarize the findings of this study in a single statement, our response would be: The process of occupational socialization during childhood has been shown to be developmental in nature, and to follow an age-related pattern largely in accord with that which has been shown or presumed to govern children's growth in general. In other words, while work itself in the formal sense may be largely a phenomenon of late adolescence and adulthood, preparation to assume one's place in the world of work and growth into an occupational self-identity begin far earlier than that.

By implication, *age* (operationalized here as grade in school) could be expected to be *the* significant independent variable in this study. And, indeed, it has been. While it would probably be inaccurate to speak very *specifically* of a *single* age-related pattern governing children's growth in awareness of the world of work, it is undoubtedly appropriate to refer to the configurations of findings presented here as "developmental."[1] That is to say, we have found in comparing groups of children at different ages that observable age-related cognitive differences are unidirectional in nature and typically differ qualitatively in terms of their levels of sophistication, abstraction, realism, etc. It is not merely that older children have more information; they also seem disposed to employ more sophisticated cognitive structures in their processing of such information.

Without resort to data gathered by means of a longitudinal design, there can be no "proof" in the strictest sense that children progress cognitively in the manner described, merely repeated observations that children of different age groups tend to be differentially distributed with respect to their tendencies to manifest certain traits. Thus, we would be overstepping ourselves were we to posit the existence of certain "stages" in the process, for our observations have been based exclusively upon cross-sectional age samples and thus, strictly speaking, must necessarily be restricted to questions of *content*, not process.

But we agree with Greenstein in his assertion that nine- and thirteen-year-olds live in many respects in different worlds.[2] In fact, we would go a step further by suggesting the applicability of certain general *descriptor terms,* if you will. On the basis of the observations presented here, it seems reasonable to suggest that children's work orientations fall into three categories, each of which may be roughly associated with an age group.

Nearly all first graders and a great many third graders surveyed here might be termed *genuinely childish* in their conceptions of the world of work. That is to say, they tend to be extremely obvious in their egocentrism, categorizing phenomena in terms of how they affect their own worlds, measure up to patently child-like standards, etc. To them, policemen are important because they help children cross streets; a great chore is brushing the cat (" 'cause she's soft"); and fifty dollars is the fortune of a lifetime. Rather than outgrow this concrete and egocentric world view all at once, we believe, most pass through what might be termed a *transitional* phase, which *seems* to encompass roughly the years from third to fifth grade. Increments in the amount of information, apparent readiness to assimilate information, degree of realism, level of conceptual complexity, tolerance for ambiguity, willingness to suspend judgment or make conditional assessments, etc., typically can be discerned during this time. While there is nothing sacred about it, fifth grade represents an apparent watershed in cognitive development with respect to work. Approximately at that point, many children arrive at a cognitive plateau. Subsequent cognitive development—at least insofar as we have been able to measure it here—seems to level off to a considerable extent. Without comparable data relating to adolescents, it is impossible to assign developmental meaning to this last phenomenon. We tentatively identify this plateau as marking entry into *embryonic adulthood,* a term which derives from our impressions (1) that the older pupils sampled manifest a number of the "seeds" of adult work orientations and (2) that they seem to have at least as much in common with adults as with children even a scant five or so years younger.

All of the above refer to cognitive development. Unfortunately, neither evaluative nor affective development can be so readily described. In part, this is because the principal focus of the study has been upon cognitive matters, relegating values and feelings to secondary positions. But more importantly, this shortcoming derives from our repeated inability to effectively isolate evaluative and affective states from the influence of cognition. Not that this is entirely regrettable: To separate values and feelings from the perceptions which underpin them would indeed be an arbitrary process, likely to result in as many distortions as additional insights.

There were of course numerous instances in which values and feelings, if not totally isolated in "pure" form, were nonetheless available to us for observation. Our general impression has been that in neither case—evaluative nor affective—is it possible to discern any clearcut developmental pattern such as that alluded to with respect to cognitive growth. While it has been established in the present investigation that both work-related feelings and values are present during early childhood, the evidence concerning their development over time must be regarded as relatively inconclusive. This in itself is interesting, however. The fact that cognitive development was so readily observable while growth (change over time) in these other aspects of children's work orientations can only be hinted at, even when values and feelings can be shown to exist, is certainly grounds for further inquiry. It may be that affective and evaluative growth, in addition to being more difficult to measure in children, lag considerably behind cognitive development.

Age was not the only variable of interest in terms of its influence upon occupational socialization. Sociologically, there was reason to believe that other demographic variables such as sex, socioeconomic status, and community of residence would be related to children's work orientations. There were suggestions of such relationships in the literature, especially with respect to the issue of occupational choice in adolescent populations. And there were indeed several instances in which sex and SES were found to be associated with observed differences in children's work-related perceptions, etc. Yet these differences were relatively small in comparison to what would have been projected, largely on the basis of the findings with respect to adolescents.

Sex differences, while numerous, were rarely of such magnitude as to support the claim that male and female children differ drastically in their *general* views of the world of work. On the other hand, on those items specifically concerned with sex-role differentiation in terms of childwork, sex-typed imagery, aspirational levels, and traditional sex-role preferences and projections, observed differences were not only consistently in predictable directions, but quite often very substantial. Moreover, the early age at which such differences are readily apparent strongly suggests that sex role differentiation receives high priority in the process of occupational socialization, and that such inculcation is most effective. Whether such differences must necessarily be considered grounds for concern or targets for reform depends in large part upon one's ideological commitments and the assumptions one is willing to make. Nor can we assess on the basis of the data at hand the extent to which such commitment to differentiated sex roles persists or fades beyond the elementary years.

Sociologists tend to expect SES differences as a matter of course in survey research. This variable, however, could hardly be said to have played an important role in our findings here. In part this may have been due to the relatively restricted range of SES differences among children in the sample. There were virtually no children of genuinely wealthy families. And there were practically none from true poverty backgrounds, since it was decided to exclude these cases when data collected revealed that their verbal skills were typically such as to render unfair most comparisons of their responses with those of working- and middle-class children. Nonetheless, two observations are possible with respect to observed SES differences in these data. In the first place, while social status was very often found not to be related to children's answers or to be only weakly associated with same, a common denominator may be discerned in several instances. That is, SES differences tended to occur with respect to items inquiring about money. Questions about how does one get money, reasons for the existence of pay differentials, savings habits, etc., elicited differential answers by SES. The observed differences were rarely very substantial. And if there is a pattern, it is not entirely clear.[3] But such findings, especially given the paucity of findings concerning SES differences in general, nonetheless suggest further inquiry into family money education practices and orientations toward money by socioeconomic status.

The other observation about SES warranted by the findings may be viewed as an attempt to reconcile many of our nonfindings with the predictions of substantial differences based upon the literature concerning adolescents. It may well be that socioeconomic status does not become a particularly important (or at least an obvious) influence upon work orientations until adolescence. We have noted in this study several instances in which SES differences, although not in evidence in the responses of first, third and fifth graders, made their appearance at the seventh grade level. Since our N's were smaller among seventh graders and not comparable to those at other levels, it was not feasible to test for interaction between grade and SES. Moreover, the observed SES differences were typically small. Such observations suggest that attention be paid in the future to the question of *when* SES differences begin to impact upon the developmental process.

Although community of residence was originally expected to be related to differences in children's work orientations, this was not in general found to be the case.

In sum, it should be stressed that age was the dominant variable in terms of influence upon children's work orientations. Even in many cases in which sex or SES proved to be associated with certain response patterns, it was only when age was controlled that such effects became discernable. Thus, we reiterate what must be considered the essential finding of the study, namely that the occupational socialization process during childhood is apparently governed by a developmental pattern.

Implications of the Findings

Having considered the findings in general, we remain confronted by a final important question: *So what?* In closing, therefore, let us turn our attention to the significance of the findings presented and to their place in the larger scheme of things. In short, let us talk of the implications of the study. First, we shall briefly discuss the sociological significance of the research, then its pragmatic implications for educational policy.

From the sociological perspective, the significance of what has been learned about children's work orientations may be summed up in terms of three key words: patterns, subcultures and attachment.

Sociology involves the search for *patterns*. Everett Hughes long ago pointed out the importance, in conducting the sociological analysis of occupations, of discovering "career lines"[4] in a generic sense, i.e., temporal, sequential, institutionalized behavioral patterns shared by those who pursue a given line of work. It is against this thinking which one must view the numerous studies of occupational activity. Such studies attempt both to extend the career approach to earlier life stages and to generalize it to include branching decisions in *any* sort of occupational track. Conceived in this tradition, this study of the development of children's work orientations has been intended to fill still another void in our knowledge of the work cycle. Starting from the assumption that career choice and specific occupational attitudes do not simply appear in late adolescence or early adulthood, this has been an effort in the documentation of childhood patterns of growth with respect to work-related knowledge, values and feelings. While there remain unanswered questions, the findings have made clear that such development not only starts early, but is far more extensive and rapid than many of us would have otherwise been prepared to believe.

Sociological investigations are often concerned with *subcultural variations* or departures from the cognitive, evaluative or affective patterns which prevail in the culture at large. We are conditioned to casually accept as reasonable statements about ethnic, criminal, or occupational subcultures, the presumption being that they do in fact refer to cultures within cultures. But what about the so-called "culture of childhood?" Do children live in a world of their own, or are they merely *homunculi* with respect to their work orientations? There is no definitive answer to this question in the context of the present investigation, but there are relevant hints. We have, for example, noted several instances in which children's definitions of situations were at variance with those usually held by adults. But such perceptions usually took the form of misconceptions or oversimplifications, and were ordinarily prominent only among our youngest respondents. Moreover, these specialized social definitions could hardly be said to derive from rejection of mainstream adult values or even lack of concern with same, merely from limitations upon children's cognitive structures or the flow of work-related information which reaches them. And by the end of elementary school, most children have at least begun to approximate adult behavioral patterns with respect to work. Put differently, the seeds of adult work orientations are apparently present early, and the ensuing development is rapid.

In light of such findings, our inclination is to view the culture of childhood approach as less than useful with respect to the analysis of children's work orientations, if only because it may prove counter-productive or misleading to future researchers. Our concern revolves around the belief that to view childhood as an essentially separate entity, as culture of childhood adherents are disposed to doing, is to run the risk of missing important developmental aspects of the social-ization process. For insights about the ultimate meaning of observed childhood behavioral patterns often flow from the necessity of recon-ciling findings with what is known of adult behavior, in an effort to discern the inherent continuity of pattern.

A more useful conceptual approach to the interpretation of our findings, we believe, has to do with the notion of *attachment*. In considering patterns above, our emphasis was largely upon the interpretation of individual behavior, i.e., upon discerning that which youthful prospective workers, and indeed all workers, have in common in terms of their passage through a generic work cycle. But another perspective is equally possible. From the standpoint of the social system, rather than individual development, it is most rele-vant to explore the question of how commitment to social institutions develops. For institutional arrangements—marriage, the family, politics, work—persist only insofar as people's attachment to them is generated and maintained. Political scientists have lead the way in this regard, probing children's embryonic attachment to various aspects of the political system. The other disciplines have been slower to take up this approach, yet there are signs of increases in such activity. It is in that context which we would prefer the present study to be viewed. That is to say, evidence has been presented which illustrates that children's work-relevant cognitions, attitudes, and feelings have much in common with those of adolescents and adults. It is hoped that future research will inquire into the connections between children's developing work orientations and subsequent behavioral issues such as work style, occupational commitment, integration into the labor force, even tendencies to be subject to alienation and other "pathologies of work."[5]

On a more pragmatic level, the findings with respect to the devel-opment of work orientations during childhood involve numerous implications, especially in the area of educational policy. While specific identification of educational needs and priorities in this regard must ultimately rest with professional educators, it would be remiss not to at least mention a few areas in which these findings might be of interest to such professionals. Arbitrarily, observations on this matter will be three kinds, focusing upon (1) the role of the educational system; (2) the role of the teacher; and (3) the provision of work opportunities for children.

School systems have long recognized, on a theoretical level, the need to incorporate occupational information into the curriculum. The matter has occupied a prominent position within the educational literature since roughly the turn of the century. The idea has been championed by eminent proponents, not the least of whom was John Dewey himself, who once wrote:[6]

> Outside of the school, a large portion of the children's plays are simply more or less miniature and haphazard attempts at reproducing social occupations . . . There are certain reasons for believing that the type of interest that springs up along with these occupations is of a healthy and really educative sort; and that by giving a larger place to occupations we should secure an excellent, perhaps the very best, way of making an appeal to the child's spontaneous interests and yet have at the same time, some guarantee that we are not dealing with what is merely pleasure-giving, exciting, or transient.

The problem has not been one of commitment, but of the translation of commitment into practical programs. Fully sixty-five years after Dewey penned those words, for example, Arbuckle could still write with justification that there was little in the educational literature dealing with the place of occupational information in the elementary school.[7] While the vast influx of federal funds in the past decade has given increased impetus to the career education movement, the situation has not changed drastically. This very project grew out of the realization in the early 1970s that there continued to exist a need for accurate information about children's work orientations. Program building in the absence of such information, it was felt, would not only run the risk of failure but could indeed prove wasteful of school resources, even counterproductive to educational aims. What was required was a foundation of empirical findings upon which could be based the assumptions which would in turn underlie curricular development and policy decisions with respect to the presentation of occupational information.

If there is a lesson for the educational community in the results of this investigation, it is this: Pay more attention to the elementary grades in the planning of programs, curricular revisions, and the allocation of resources for the purpose of influencing children's

occupational orientations. Perhaps the single most important observation that may be gleaned from these findings is that the vast
majority of development in children's work orientations is well under
way before the end of the elementary years. Nor are we alone in
making such an assessment: others investigating children's growth
in awareness of the social world, including the world of work, have
noted a similar pattern.[8] The implication is clear: To wait until junior
high school or beyond to begin attempting to influence children's
occupational development is to miss an important period of opportunity. It may also necessitate the introduction of programs to facilitate
un-learning or re-learning of previously developed perceptions,
attitudes, and values which educators may regard as not in students'
best interests. As we know, remedial programs are not only costly,
but historically they have been relatively ineffective.

It has been pointed out that the social and economic impetus for
career education derives from disappointment with labor market
performance of youthful products of our educational institutions,
concern over the apparent rise in job dissatisfaction/motivational
problems (as reflected in absenteeism, increases in public assistance
rolls, etc.), and concern with whether increased productivity can be
made to keep pace with social change in general in this country.[9]
Such concerns suggest the conviction that all is not well in the
American world of work and, beyond that, a notion that schools have
some responsibility to remedy the situation in the long run. Whether
such beliefs are accurate or realistic is not our concern here. The point
is that if educators do sense such an obligation, they would do well to
attend closely to empirical findings such as those presented here.

Closely related to the question of system response in the face of
such information is the notion of individual teacher reaction. While
teachers must be viewed as agents of the educational system, it would
be wrong to overlook the autonomy exercised by many of them in
their own classrooms. "Good elementary educators," as Hoyt et al.
have pointed out, "have always provided their students with some
awareness of the world of work. Others have added innovations as the
concern for career education has risen. *More are willing but do not
know how.*"[10] Such assessment may be a trifle credulous. Certainly it
is also true, as a 1962 study in the Detroit school system suggested,
that teachers may play down vocational courses, perpetuating the
dichotomy between work-related and "academic" information in the
school.[11] In any event, the role of the teacher in implementing career
education programs is certainly problematic. If it is true that teachers have been reluctant to emphasize occupational information in the

absence of evidence relating age norms and baseline information, it is hoped that these findings will prove helpful.

Our final observation does not necessarily relate to educational policy, although it could certainly be interpreted in that light. Goodwin, in his study of work orientations among young persons of poverty backgrounds, explained the deterioration of positive work values on the basis of an imperfect opportunity structure which offered little chance for potentially confidence-building work experience.[12] Here we have noted the generally positive feelings among child workers with respect to their chores or jobs. But such experiences are neither assured to every child nor guaranteed to be particularly positive in nature. Thus, in closing, we would like to raise the question of institutionalizing childwork in some manner. This is not by any means to propose the repeal of the child labor statutes. But in view of the findings with respect to children's development of work orientations it is suggested that consideration be given, perhaps through the "natural" medium of the school, to providing at least those children who do not otherwise receive it the opportunity to gain work experience in as favorable an environment as possible.

Notes

1. It is acknowledged that "developmental" patterns, in the strictest and most formal sense of the word can only be documented with the use of a longitudinal research design. This was not possible here. For an extended and more precise discussion of the criteria involved in assessing developmental patterns, see: Lawrence Kohlberg, "Stage and Sequence: The Cognitive-Developmental Approach to Socialization," in *Handbook of Socialization Theory and Research,* ed. David A. Goslin (Chicago: Rand McNally, 1969), pp. 347-480. (See especially, pp. 352-356.)

2. Fred I. Greenstein, *Children and Politics* (New Haven, Conn.: Yale University Press, 1965), pp. 1-2.

3. Borow in his review of the literature on occupational socialization noted that the impact of social class was not clear. See: Henry Borow, "Development of Occupational Motives and Roles," in *Review of Child Development Research,* vol. II, ed. L. W. Hoffman and M. L. Hoffman, (New York: Russell Sage Foundation, 1966), p. 413.

4. Everett C. Hughes, *The Sociological Eye: Selected Papers on Work, Self, and the Study of Society,* vol. II (Chicago: Aldine, 1971), pp. 405-406.

5. For an expanded discussion of the various "pathologies of work," see: Thomas F. Green, "Career Education and the Pathologies of Work," in *Essays on Career Education* ed. Larry McClure and Carolyn Buan (Portland, Ore.: Northwest Regional Educational Laboratory, 1973), pp. 207-220.

6. John Dewey, *The School and Society* (Chicago: University of Chicago Press, 1899), p. 135.

7. Dugald S. Arbuckle, "Occupational Information in the Elementary School," *Vocational Guidance Quarterly* 12 (Winter 1963-64), pp. 77-84.

8. Studies by Chaney, Kuldau and Hollis, and Dennis, to name just a few, have all suggested that children level off in terms of their development by the end of elementary school, if not earlier. See: Reece Chaney, "Vocational Values of Children as They Relate to Economic Community, Grade Level, Sex, and Parental Occupational Level" (unpublished Ph.D. dissertation, Ohio University, 1968); Joyce E. Kuldau and Joseph W. Hollis, "The Development of Attitudes Toward Work Among Upper Elementary School Age Children," *Journal of Vocational Behavior* 1 (October 1971), pp. 387-398; Jack Dennis, *Political Learning in Childhood and Adolescence: A Study of Fifth, Eighth, and Eleventh Graders in Milwaukee, Wisconsin* (Madison, Wisc.: University of Wisconsin Research and Development Center for Cognitive Learning, 1969).

9. Kenneth B. Hoyt, Nancy M. Pinson, Darryl Laramore, and Garth L. Mangum, *Career Education and the Elementary School Teacher* (Salt Lake City: Olympus Publishing Co., 1973) pp. 9-11.

10. Ibid., p. 9 (emphasis added).

11. "Preparing Pupils for the World of Work" (Detroit: Detroit Public School System, 1962).

12. Leonard Goodwin, *Do the Poor Want to Work?* (Washington, D.C.: Brookings Institution, 1972).

Bibliography

Allport, Gordon W., *The Nature of Prejudice.* Garden City, N.Y.: Anchor Books, 1958.

Appleton, George M., and Hanson, James C. "Parent Child Relations, Need Nurturance, and Vocational Orientation." *Personnel and Guidance Journal* 47 (April 1969): 794-799.

Arbuckle, Dugald S. "Occupational Information in the Elementary School." *Vocational Guidance Quarterly* 12 (Winter 1963-1964): 77-84.

Aries, Philippe. *Centuries of Childhood: A Social History of Family Life.* Translated by Robert Baldick. New York: Vintage Books, 1965.

Aronowitz, Stanley. *False Promises: The Shaping of American Working Class Consciousness.* New York: McGraw-Hill, 1973.

Bandura, Albert. "Social Learning Theory of Identification Processes." In *Handbook of Socialization Theory and Research,* pp. 213-262. Edited by David A. Goslin. Chicago: Rand McNally, 1969.

Baron, Robert A.; Byrne, Donn; and Griffitt, William. *Social Psychology: Understanding Human Interaction.* Boston: Allyn and Bacon, 1974.

Benoit-Smullyan, Emile. "Status, Status Types, and Status Interrelations." *American Sociological Review* 9 (April 1944): 154-161.

Berg, Ivar. " 'They Won't Work': The End of the Protestant Ethic and All That." In *Work and the Quality of Life: Resource Papers for Work in America*, pp. 27-38. Edited by James O'Toole. Cambridge, Massachusetts: M.I.T. Press, 1974.

Berger, Peter L., ed. "Some General Observations on the Problem of Work." *The Human Shape of Work*, pp. 211-241. New York: MacMillan and Co., 1964.

Blalock, Hubert M. *Social Statistics*. New York: McGraw-Hill, 1960.

Blau, Peter M., and Duncan, Otis Dudley. *The American Occupational Structure*. New York: John Wiley and Sons, 1967.

Borow, Henry. "Development of Occupational Motives and Roles." In *Review of Child Development Research*, Vol. II, pp. 373-422. Edited by L. W. Hofman and M. L. Hoffman. New York: Russell Sage Foundation, 1966.

Borow, Henry. "An Integral View of Occupational Theory and Research." In *Man in a World of Work*, pp. 364-386. Edited by Henry Borow. Boston: Houghton-Mifflin, 1964.

Brown, Roger. *Social Psychology*. New York: Free Press, 1965.

Buehler, C. *Der Menschliche Lebenslauf auf Psychologisches Problem*. Leipzig: Herzel, 1933.

Byrne, Donn, and Clore, Gerald L. "A Reinforcement Model of Evaluative Responses." *Personality: An International Journal* 1 (Summer 1970): 103-128.

Chaney, Reece. "Vocational Values of Children as They Relate to Economic Community, Grade, Level, Sex, and Parental Occupational Level." Ph.D. dissertation, Ohio University, 1968.

Chenowith, Lawrence. *The American Dream of Success*. North Scituate, Mass.: Duxbury Press, 1974.

Chinoy, Ely. *Automobile Workers and the American Dream*. New York: Random House, 1955.

Connell, R. W. *The Child's Construction of Politics*. Melbourne, Australia: Melbourne University Press, 1971.

Cremin, Lawrence A. *The Transformation of the School: Progressivism in American Education*. New York: Random House, 1964.

Crites, John O. "Parental Identification in Relation to Vocational Interest Development." *Journal of Educational Psychology* 53 (December 1962): 262-270.

Danziger, Kurt. "Children's Earliest Conceptions of Economic Relationships." *Journal of Social Psychology* 47 (May 1958): 231-234.

Davies, A. F. "The Child's Discovery of Nationality." *Australian and New Zealand Journal of Sociology* 4 (October 1968): 107-125.

Davis, Kingsly, and Moore, Wilbert E. "Some Principles of Stratification." *American Sociological Review* 10 (April 1945): 242-249.

DeFleur, Lois B. "Ascending Occupational Knowledge in Young Children." *Sociological Inquiry* 36 (Winter 1966): 98-115.

DeGrazia, Sebastian. *Of Time, Work, and Leisure.* Garden City, N.Y.: Doubleday, 1964.

Dennis, Jack. *Political Learning in Childhood and Adolescence: A Study of Fifth, Eighth, and Eleventh Grades in Milwaukee, Wisconsin.* Madison, Wisc.: University of Wisconsin Research and Development Center for Cognitive Learning, 1969.

Detroit Public School System. *Preparing Pupils for the World of Work.* Detroit: Detroit Public School System, 1962.

Dewey, John. *The School and Society.* Chicago: University of Chicago Press, 1899.

Dowse, Robert E., and Hughes, John. "The Family, the School, and the Political Socialization Process." *Sociology* 5 (January 1971): 21-46.

Drucker, Peter. *Management: Tasks, Responsibilities, Practices.* New York: Harper and Row, 1973.

Dyer, William G. "Parental Influence on the Job Attitudes of Children from Two Occupational Strata." *Sociology and Social Research* 42 (January-February 1958): 203-206.

Easton, David, and Dennis, Jack. *Children in the Political System.* New York: McGraw-Hill, 1969.

Easton, David, and Hess, Robert D. "The Child's Political World." *Midwest Journal of Political Science* 6 (August 1962): 229-246.

Elkin, Fred. *The Child and Society.* New York: Random House, 1960.

Emmerich, Walter W. "Young Children's Discrimination of Parent and Child Roles." *Child Development* 30 (September 1959): 403-419.

Engel, Mary; Marsden, Gerald; and Woodman, Sylvia. "Children Who Work and the Concept of Work Styles." *Psychiatry* 30 (November 1967): 392-404.

Engel, Mary; Marsden, Gerald; and Woodman, Sylvia. "Orientation to Work in Children." *American Journal of Orthopsychiatry* 38 (January 1968): 137-143.

Erikson, Erik H. *Childhood and Society.* New York: W. W. Norton and Co., 1963.

Festinger, Leon A. *A Theory of Cognitive Dissonance.* New York: Row, Peterson, 1957.

Festinger, Leon; Riecken, Henry W.; and Schachler, Stanley. *When Prophecy Fails.* New York: Harper and Row, 1956.

Freeston, P. M. "Vocational Interests in Elementary School Children." *Occupational Psychology* 13 (July 1939): 223-237.

Gans, Herbert. *The Levittowners.* New York: Random House, 1967.

Gans, Herbert. *The Urban Villagers.* New York: Free Press, 1962.

Ginzberg, Eli; Ginsberg, S. W.; Axelrod, S.; and Herma, J. L. *Occupational Choice: An Approach to a General Theory.* New York: Columbia University Press, 1951.

Ginzberg, Eli. "Toward a Theory of Occupational Choice: A Restatement." *Vocational Guidance Quarterly* 20 (March 1972): 169-176.

Goodman, Mary Ellen. *The Culture of Childhood: Child's Eye View of Society and Culture.* New York: Teachers College Press, 1970.

Goodwin, Leonard. *Do the Poor Want to Work: A Social-Psychological Study of Work Orientations.* Washington, D.C.: Brookings Institution, 1972.

Gouldner, Alvin W. "The Norm of Reciprocity: A Preliminary Statement." *American Sociological Review* 25 (April 1960): 161-178.

Green, Thomas F. "Career Education and the Pathologies of Work." In *Essays on Career Education,* pp. 207-220. Edited by Larry McClure and Carolyn Buan. Portland, Ore.: Northwest Regional Educational Laboratory, 1973.

Greenberg, Edward S. "Black Children and the Political System: A Study of Socialization to Support." *Public Opinion Quarterly* 34 (Fall 1970): 333-345.

Greenstein, Fred I. *Children and Politics.* New Haven, Conn.: Yale University Press, 1965.

Greenstein, Fred I. "The Benevolent Leader: Children's Images of Political Authority." *American Political Science Review* 54 (December 1960): 934-943.

Gunn, Barbara, "Children's Conceptions of Occupational Prestige." *Personnel and Guidance Journal* 52 (February 1964): 558-563.

Haire, Mason, and Morrison, Florence. "School Children's Perceptions of Labor and Management." *Journal of Social Psychology* 44 (November 1967): 179-197.

Harris, Dale B.; Clark, Kenneth E.; Rose, Arnold M.; and Valasek, Frances. "The Relationship of Children's Home Duties to Responsibilities." *Child Development* 25 (March 1954): 29-33.

Hartley, Ruth E. "Children's Conceptions of Male and Female Roles." *Merrill-Palmer Quarterly* 6 (Summer-Fall 1960): 83-91.

Hartley, Ruth E. "Sex-Role Pressures and the Socialization of the Male Child." *Psychological Reports* 5 (September 1959): 457-468.

Hartup, W. W. "Some Correlates of Parental Imitation in Young Children." *Child Development* 38 (March 1962): 85-97.

Havigurst, Robert J. "Youth in Exploration and Man Emergent." In *Man in a World at Work,* pp. 215-236. Edited by Henry Borow. Boston: Houghton-Mifflin, 1964.

Hess, Robert, and Torney, Judith V. *The Development of Political Attitudes in Children.* Garden City, N.Y.: Doubleday-Anchor Books, 1968.

Hollingshead, August B. "A Two-Factor Index of Social Position." New Haven, Conn.: Yale University Press, 1957. (Mimeographed.)

Hollingshead, August B., and Redlich, Frederick. *Social Class and Mental Illness.* New York: John Wiley and Sons, 1958.

Horner, Mattina S. "Achievement-Related Conflicts in Women." *Journal of Social Issues* 28 (Number 2 1972): 157-175.

Hoyt, Kenneth B.; Pinson, Nancy M.; Laramore, Darryl; and Mangum, Garth L. *Career Education and the Elementary School Teacher.* Salt Lake City: Olympus Publishing Co., 1973.

Hughes, Everett C. *The Sociological Eye: Selected Papers on Work, Self, and the Study of Society,* Vol. II. Chicago: Aldine, 1971.

Hyman, Herbert H. *Political Socialization: A Study in the Psychology of Political Behavior.* Glencoe, Ill.: Free Press, 1959.

Jaros, Dean. *Socialization to Politics.* New York, Praeger Publishing Co., 1973.

Keller, Suzanne. *The Urban Neighborhood: A Sociological Perspective.* New York: Random House, 1968.

Kohlberg, Lawrence. "Stage and Sequence: The Cognitive-Developmental Approach to Socialization." In *Handbook of Socialization Theory and Research,* pp. 347-480. Edited by David A. Goslin. Chicago: Rand McNally, 1969.

Kuldau, Joyce E., and Hollis, Joseph W. "The Development of Attitudes Toward Work Among Upper Elementary School Age Children." *Journal of Vocational Behavior* 1 (October 1971): 387-398.

Lambert, William, and Klineberg, Otto. "Cultural Comparisons of Boys' Occupational Aspirations." *British Journal of Social and Clinical Psychology* 3 (February 1963): 56-65.

Laver, Robert H. "Socialization into Inequality: Children's Perceptions of Occupational Status." *Sociology and Social Research* 58 (January 1974): 176-183.

Leighton, Dorothy, and Kluckholn, Clyde. *Children of the People: The Navaho and His Development.* Cambridge, Mass.: Harvard University, 1947.

Lenski, Gerhard. "A Theoretical Synthesis." In *Social Stratification: A Reader,* pp. 75-86. Edited by Joseph Lopreato and Lionel S.

Lewis. New York: Harper and Row, 1974.

Lenski, Gerhard. *Power and Privilege.* New York: McGraw-Hill, 1966.

Liebow, Elliot. *Tally's Corner: A Study of Negro Street Corner Men.* Boston: Little, Brown, 1967.

Lipsman, Claire. "Maslow's Theory of Needs in Relation to Vocational Choice by Students from Lower Socio-Economic Levels." *Vocational Guidance Quarterly* 15 (June 1967): 283-288.

Looft, William R. "Vocational Aspirations of Second Grade Girls." *Psychological Reports* 28 (February 1971): 241-242.

Lopreato, Joseph, and Lewis, Lionel, eds. *Social Stratification: A Reader.* New York: Harper and Row, 1974.

Maas, Jeanette, and Michael, William B. "The Relationship of Interest Choices of Kindergarten Children to Social Group Membership and to Sex Differences." *California Journal of Educational Research* 15 (January 1964): 24-33.

Maccoby, Eleanor E. "Class Differences in Boys' Choices of Authority Roles." *Sociometry* 25 (March 1962): 117-119.

Maccoby, Eleanor E. "Role Taking in Childhood and its Consequences for Social Learning." *Child Development* 30 (June 1959): 239-252.

Marland, Sidney P. Foreword to *Essays on Career Education,* pp. vii-xi. Edited by Larry McClure and Carolyn Buan. Portland, Ore.: Northwest Regional Educational Laboratory, 1973.

Marshall, Helen R., and Magruder, Lucille. "Relations Between Parent Money Practices and Children's Knowledge and Use of Money." *Child Development* 31 (June 1960): 253-284.

Marx, Karl. *Selected Writings in Sociology and Social Philosophy.* Translated by T. B. Bottomore. New York: McGraw-Hill, 1956.

Merton, Robert K. *Social Theory and Social Structure.* New York: Free Press, 1968.

Miller, Delbert C., and Form, William H. *Industrial Sociology.* New York: Harper, 1951.

Miller, Louise B.; Dyer, Jean L.; and Biber, Henry. *Experimental Variables of Head Start Curricula: A Comparison of Current Approaches: Annual Progress Report.* Louisville, Ky.: University of Louisville, 1970.

Moore, Wilbert E. "Occupational Socialization," *Handbook of Socialization Theory and Research,* pp. 861-882. Edited by David A. Goslin. Chicago: Rand McNally, 1969.

Morris, Richard T., and Murphy, Raymond J. "The Situs Dimension of Occupational Structure." *American Sociological Review* 24 (April 1959): 231-239.

National Opinion Research Center. "Jobs and Occupations: A Popular Evaluation." *Opinion News* 9 (September 1947): 3-13.

New Jersey State Department of Education, Division of Educational Statistics. *Annual Report of the New Jersey Commissioner of Education.* Trenton, N.J.: New Jersey State Department of Education, 1971.

Orum, Anthony M., and Cohen, Roberta S. "The Development of Political Orientations Among Black and White Children." *American Sociological Review* 38 (February 1973): 62-74.

Orwell, George. *Animal Farm.* New York: Harcourt, Brace, and World, Inc., 1964.

Parker, Harry J. "29,000 Seventh Graders Have Made Occupational Choices." *Vocational Guidance Quarterly* 11 (Autumn 1962): 54-55.

Piaget, Jean. *The Child's Conception of the World.* New York: Harcourt and Brace, 1959.

Piaget, Jean, and Weil, A. M. "The Development in Children of the Idea of Homeland, and of Relations with other Countries." *International Social Science Bulletin* 3 (Autumn 1951): 561-578.

Rawls, John. *A Theory of Justice.* Cambridge, Mass.: Harvard University Press, 1971.

Reiss, Albert J. Jr.; Duncan, Otis Dudley; Hatt, Paul K.; and North, Cecil C. *Occupational and Social Status.* Glencoe, Ill.: Free Press, 1961.

Robinson, John P.; Athanasiou, Robert; and Head, Kendra B., eds. *Measure of Occupational Characteristics.* Ann Arbor, Mich.: Institute for Social Research, University of Michigan, 1969.

Roe, Anne. "Perspectives on Vocational Development." In *Perspectives on Vocational Development,* pp. 61-82. Edited by John M. Whitely and Arthur Resnikoff. Washington, D.C.: American Personnel and Guidance Association, 1972.

Roe, Anne. *The Psychology of Occupations.* New York: John Wiley and Sons, 1956.

Rosen, Bernard C. "Race, Ethnicity, and the Achievement Syndrome." *American Sociological Review* 24 (February 1959): 47-60.

Rosenthal, Robert, and Jacobson, Lenore. *Pygmalion in the Classroom.* New York: Holt, Rinehart, and Winston, 1968.

Roethlisberger, Frank J., and Dickson, William. *Management and the Worker.* Cambridge, Mass.: Harvard University Press, 1939.

Schlossberg, N. K., and Goodman, J. "A Women's Place: Children's Sex Stereotyping of Occupations." *Vocational Guidance Quarterly* 20 (June 1972): 266-270.

Schuessler, Karl, and Strauss, Anselm L. "A Study of Concept Learning by Scale Analysis." *American Sociological Review* 15 (December 1950): 752-762.

Siegal, Sidney. *Nonparametric Statistics for the Behavioral Sciences.* New York: McGraw-Hill, 1956.

Simmons, Dale D. "Children's Rankings of Occupational Prestige." *Personnel and Guidance Journal* 41 (December 1962): 332-336.

Simmons, Roberta G., and Rosenberg, Morris. "Functions of Children's Perceptions of the Stratification System." *American Sociological Review* 36 (April 1971): 235-249.

Smith, Robert, and Proshansky, Harold. *Conceptions of Work, Play, Competence and Occupation in Junior and Senior High School Students: Final Report.* (Ann Arbor, Mich.: University of Michigan Institute for Social Research, [1967]).

Sorenson, A. G., and Morris, Irma. "Attitudes and Beliefs as Sources of Vocational Preference." *Journal of Educational Research* 51 (September 1962): 20-27.

Special Task Force to the Secretary of Health, Education, and Welfare. *Work in America.* Cambridge, Mass.: M.I.T. Press, 1973.

Spradley, James P. "Career Education in Cultural Perspective." In *Essays in Career Education,* pp. 11-16. Edited by Larry McClure and Carolyn Buan. Portland, Ore.: Northwest Regional Educational Laboratory, 1973.

Stendler, Celis B. *Children of Brasstown.* Urbana, Ill.: University of Illinois Press, 1949.

Strauss, Anselm L. "The Development and Transformation of Monetary Meanings in the Child." *American Sociological Review* 17 (June 1952): 257-286.

Super, Donald E. "Consistency and Wisdom of Vocational Maturity in Ninth Grade." *Journal of Educational Psychology* 52 (February 1961): 35-43.

Super, Donald E., and Bachrach, Paul B. *Vocational Development: A Framework of Research.* New York: Columbia University Press, 1957.

Terkel, Studs. *Hard Times.* New York: Avon Books, 1970.

Terkel, Studs. *Working.* New York: Avon Books, 1972.

Thomas, William I., and Thomas, Dorothy Swaine. *The Child in America.* New York: Knopf, 1928.

Tilgher, Adriano. *Homo Faber: Work Through the Ages.* Translated by Dorothy Canfield Fisher. Chicago: Henry Regnery Co., 1958.

Tischin, Moses, ed. *The American Gospel of Success.* Chicago: Quadrangle Books, 1965.

Tumin, Melvin M. "Some Principles of Stratification: A Critical Analysis." *American Sociological Review* 18 (August 1953): 387-393.

Turner, Ralph. *The Social Context of Ambition.* San Francisco: Chandler Publishing Co., 1964.

Tyler, Leona E. "The Development of Vocational Interests I: The Organization of Likes and Dislikes in Ten-Year-Old Children." *Journal of Genetic Psychology* 86 (March 1955): 33-44.

U.S. Census Bureau. *Money Income in 1971 of Families and Persons in the United States.* Series p-60, no. 85. Washington, D.C.: U.S. Government Printing Office, 1972.

U.S. Census Bureau. *Social and Economic Characteristics of New Jersey, 1970.* Washington, D.C.: U.S. Census Bureau, 1970.

Weber, Max. *The Protestant Ethic and the Spirit of Capitalism.* Translated by Talcott Parsons. New York: Charles Scribner's Sons, 1958.

Weinstein, Eugene A. "Children's Conceptions of Occupational Stratification." *Sociology and Social Research* 42 (March-April 1958): 278-284.

Weinstein, Eugene A. "Weights Assigned by Children to Criteria of Prestige." *Sociometry* 14 (June 1956): 126-132.

Williams, Joyce W. "A Gradient of Economic Concepts of Elementary Children and Factors Associated with Cogniton." Ph.D. dissertation Florida State University, 1969.

Williams, L. K. "Measurement of Risk-Taking Propensity in Industrial Settings." Ph.D. dissertation, University of Michigan, 1960.

Williams, Robin M. Jr. *American Society.* New York: Alfred A. Knopf, 1957.

Zajonc, Robert. "Cognitive Structure and Cognitive Tuning." Ph.D. dissertation, University of Michigan, 1955.

Index